T0354403

THE RIGHT PATH

Life After Death

Saoirse Brown

BALBOA.
PRESS

A DIVISION OF HAY HOUSE

Contents

Balboa Press books may be ordered through booksellers or by contacting:

Balboa Press
A Division of Hay House
1663 Liberty Drive
Bloomington, IN 47403
www.balboapress.com
1 (877) 407-4847

Print information available on the last page.

ISBN: 978-1-9822-1379-4 (sc)
ISBN: 978-1-9822-1378-7 (hc)
ISBN: 978-1-9822-1380-0 (e)

Library of Congress Control Number: 2018911872

Balboa Press rev. date: 10/12/2018

In Loving Memory
of
Richard Howorth

He is not lost forever
But just for a while
We will meet him again
And experience that smile

Angels of the Light

There is nothing to be afraid of I can promise that
Keep moving forward, no need to look back
Follow your path, where you are guided to be
Your heart will take you to your true destiny

Acknowledgments

████ ████ ████ ████ ████ ████ ████ ████ ████ ████ ████ ████

The Right Path would not exist without the help of others.

Although I was determined to tell my story, I procrastinated about writing this book for many months until I was guided to research for an editor to help with documenting my story. The search took all but a couple of minutes when Teena Lyons, former *Mail on Sunday* journalist, was gently suggested to me as the person to help me do just that. I just had to convince her to accept my unusual story. Heartfelt gratitude goes to Teena. Her expertise was invaluable with the creation of this book.

I would also like to thank the exceptional staff at Balboa Press for putting my story to paper and for all their help with the marketing of the book.

Much love must go to my guides and angels. They all guided me through this difficult process, standing by me and encouraging me all along the way. They even helped by showing me the title of this book.

I would like to give heartfelt thanks to all of staff at the Royal Marsden Hospital, including the wonderful support we received from the MacMillan nurses. I am also eternally grateful to the district nurses and the Princess Alice Hospice nurses, who all worked so hard to make Richard's final days comfortable.

I am grateful to my siblings, Jackie, Kenny, Sonia, John, Dawn, and Stephen, for their continued love and support. (I include my brother-in-law, Kenny, and sister-in-law, Dawn, as siblings and rightly so.) They have all kept me sane through this process, and I can't emphasize enough how crucial my wonderful family has been and continues to be to me. Thanks too to all of my dear friends who have stood by my side even though at times I may have sounded a little crazy.

The biggest thanks of all go to my amazing children, Ellie and Jack. I have such enduring love and admiration for them both. They have consistently shown strength and maturity through their tragic loss and beyond. I know it hasn't been easy, but I also know that their father would be very proud of them, as am I.

Finally, of course, to my wonderful husband, Richard, who has shown me that life doesn't end with death. He was always an inspiration in life, and now he has passed he continues to inspire me to help others every single day. I cannot stop people going through difficult times when they lose a loved one, but thanks to Richard, I can help them and show that the end is actually only ever the beginning of something very, very special.

Introduction

Nobody really thinks about death until they have to. Yet, when we lose someone we love, it is usual to begin questioning, "What next?" Is there a heaven? Is there an afterlife?

This is a story of my unusual journey over the past two years. It began with the untimely death of my beloved and treasured husband, Richard. Not long after his passing, I began to experience things of a spiritual nature.

Always having described myself as spiritually aware but not spiritually awake, I very soon had to question everything I had ever known about this universe.

I decided to write this book to reveal my truth on the subject. I hope my story will be a source of comfort—firstly, for anybody going through grief and, secondly, for anybody experiencing spiritual awakening symptoms, which can be very frightening.

To begin with, I was worried about how this book would be interpreted. I speculated that others would assume that my profound grief has affected my judgement. However, when you arrive at the place I am in, acceptance and approval mean nothing. In my situation, I have no option but to move forward with purpose. Besides, as you will see, allowing myself to stay in the spiritual closet is no longer an option. There are some powerful voices urging me to speak out.

Throughout my journey, I have found peace and happiness. It is my duty to share with you how this personal enrichment was achieved during one of the hardest periods of my life.

Welcome to my story.

Chapter 1

CHANGES

It doesn't look good.

Just four words. Four little words. Four little words that took everything I loved and held dear and crushed it into a million pieces.

It doesn't look good.

My head was spinning as a wave of panic surged through my body. I willed myself to look calm and matter-of-fact as I stole a glance at Rick who was sitting rigid and expressionless in the chair beside me. The only hint at his reaction was that the color had completely drained from his face.

I reached out and put my hand on his knee. Rick continued to stare straight ahead at the doctor seated behind the large desk that divided us.

"As it is now late on Friday evening, we will need to wait until Monday to get the full results of the blood tests and the endoscopy," the doctor intoned.

He began shuffling paperwork on his desk. I sensed he wanted us to go. It was getting late. Most of the other departments had already closed, and staff were quickly exiting the building. Yet Rick and I didn't move. We were waiting for the punchline.

But I am sure there is nothing to worry about.

The punchline never came.

Finally, with the awkward silence enveloping us, we got to our feet and walked outside. Neither of us said a word as we stumbled to our car. As we passed the reception area, a nurse was chatting loudly with the woman seated behind the large desk. Just as we passed, the receptionist let out a hoot of laughter at her friend's joke.

How can you be laughing at a time like this? I thought. *Just how?*

The car park was half-full. It was a private hospital, and most of the day patients had no doubt long gone home and were looking forward to a weekend with their families. We found our car, and Rick clicked the key fob to unlock the door. I slipped into the passenger seat, my heart still thumping.

"Don't worry. I'm sure it is nothing," Rick said. He wasn't looking at me. He was staring ahead, his hands gripping the top of the steering wheel tightly. So tightly, in fact, his knuckles were almost white.

I swallowed hard. I knew I needed to say something but didn't know what. In our relationship, Rick had always been the more upbeat one—the glass-half-full type. Somehow, he'd found the positive in everything. I was the one who always took a serious approach, while Rick kept his childlike manner. If anyone ever did or said something negative to me, he'd jump right in and tell me it wasn't meant in that way.

Now it was my turn to return the compliment. Except I couldn't speak.

"I told you we should have gone on that trip around Europe before visiting the doctor," Rick said at last with a faint smile as he started the car and gunned the engine.

As we drove through the lanes in the fading light, I just kept going over and over what the doctor had said. I could still see him sitting in front of me, a short, dark-haired man with a serious expression as his brown eyes blinked behind his half-moon glasses.

It doesn't look good.

As I replayed it over and over, I realized with a start there was something more—something that had sent my battered emotions into free fall. It wasn't just the words the doctor had said. He'd also held my gaze for a fraction of second longer than necessary. It was barely perceptible if I hadn't been looking for it, or thinking about it, but in that moment, I recalled it. My blood almost froze. His expression seemed to be saying: brace yourself.

How had this happened? Just a day before we'd been as happy and carefree as ever, and then—*boom*—our whole world had shattered.

I felt a pang of guilt. Rick had only gone to the doctor because I had made him. He hadn't wanted to come to England at all. He was quite happy to stay in our home in Abu Dhabi, enjoying the sunshine and catching up with a game of golf after work. The light evenings and perpetual warm weather always allowed for a quick hit of a few balls to relax.

"You go with the kids," he'd said over and over again leading up to the trip. "You know I hate England. It's always so cold and wet. It's depressing."

It had been the same every year since we'd moved to the Gulf States for Rick's job as a driller on the oil rigs. Eighteen years we'd spent out there, traveling around various areas: Doha, Qatar, Bahrain, Dubai; and, most recently, Abu Dhabi, where we had settled a couple of times. We always seemed to be drawn back to Abu Dhabi. Our kids, Ellie, now twenty, and Jack, nineteen, had grown up there. I loved our life out there but also wanted to come home each year to see friends and family.

Mind you, after weeks of arguing with Rick to make the annual trip, I'd have virtually the same conversation with everyone in the UK when we visited.

"Why would you ever leave Abu Dhabi?" they'd ask incredulously. "You're so lucky to live there!"

They were right too. Our lives out there were perfect. Nothing needed to change. We'd spend careless weekends speeding around in our boat in the calm blue waters of the Persian Gulf. Sometimes we'd hunt for dolphins, squealing with delight when we found them and they'd swim effortlessly alongside us. None of us ever lost the thrill of seeing these beautiful creatures up close. On one occasion, I encountered a heartbreaking scene. I saw two adult dolphins swimming together, and one of the adults was carrying the lifeless form of a young dolphin. The mother was in mourning, unwilling to let go of her calf, they continue to do this for days until complete exhaustion takes over and they have no other option but to let go. Luckily, I only encountered anything this tragic once. On every other occasion, we were greeted with playful dolphins, jumping in and out of the water, as if they were putting on a show just for us.

In fact, when my father, Bill, had visited, he had laughed and said that he had paid a fortunate to go dolphin spotting on previous holidays, yet had never seen a single one. Here, though, you could barely avoid them. On other days, we'd just while away the hours going nowhere in particular, gazing at the billionaire super yachts sailing self-importantly around the bay. Rick always liked to look out for the deserted islands too, perhaps dreaming of building a sumptuous retreat on one. We'd always end the day with a barbecue on the beaches, feeling the golden sand beneath our bare feet, relishing the warmth and beauty of the setting sun.

Weekdays were luxurious too. Rick's earnings were tax-free, so we wanted for nothing, in light of our financial situation Rick preferred that I didn't work. I looked after the kids, and when they were at school, I busied myself with preparing for one of our regular entertaining events or enjoying a leisurely life looking after myself and Rick when he came in from work. We had a traditional marriage, and it worked well for us both. Our social life was always busy with plenty of friends. Most of them were expats like us. Everyone loved Rick, with his warm, effervescent personality. He was always the life and soul of every party, keeping everyone laughing with a string of hilarious stories, where as I would take more of a back seat.

It was easy to see how he had done so well in life. He'd literally started at the bottom with his career on the rigs. When we'd first met in a bar in Scunthorpe, he was what was known as a roustabout, which is the person who is responsible for the basic cleaning of an oil rig—a general dog's body really. That was Rick's description anyhow. By sheer force of personality, coupled with a lot of hard graft, he worked his way up to become assistant driller, then driller, and then drilling superintendent.

I'm not sure when it was that we first realized something wasn't quite right. He just started feeling a little more tired than usual. I'd often joked that he looked a bit like Paul Hollywood of *Great British Bake Off* fame with his goatee beard and short salt-and-pepper hair, although Rick's eyes were brown, not blue like the TV chef's. Now, though, Rick had developed dark rings below his eyes. He was tired, and instead of being the first to say yes whenever anyone suggested a night out, he'd say he'd rather stay in. Yet, even though he was constantly tired, he was not sleeping well.

I was convinced it was because he had been working too hard. He just needed a break. Fortunately, work was slowing down for a while, so I introduced the idea of him taking a two-month sabbatical.

"It will give you some time to relax and enjoy some much-needed time with the kids," I suggested. "You can catch up with our friends, recharge your batteries over a few games of golf, and go back to work feeling refreshed."

"Is this your new tactic to persuade me to go home?" he said suspiciously. "You know my thoughts on that."

Fortunately, he seemed to be smiling, so I pressed my advantage.

"We don't have to spend the entire time in Surrey. We could—I don't know—take a driving trip around Europe. Take in some of the cities we've always talked about seeing."

Now I had him. We'd not long ago bought a new Aston Martin, and I knew he was dying to give it a long run. The prospect of being able to drive on the German Autobahn, with no speed restrictions, was too tempting to miss.

"All right." He nodded. "But the minimum possible time in the UK. Got it?"

"Yeah, yeah," I said, smiling.

I couldn't wait for the trip. It wasn't very often that I got him back to the UK where we could both enjoy socializing with friends. When we first moved into our property in Surrey, the neighbors would joke that I had an imaginary marriage because Rick never came home. It was always just me and the children.

We were just a few weeks away from leaving Abu Dhabi when Rick first started complaining that something wasn't right. He'd started coughing during an evening meal and didn't seem to be able to stop. We were over in Bahrain, enjoying dinner at Rick's favorite restaurant, The Meat Co. We spent so much time there that the restaurant owners eventually had two steak knives made with our names engraved on them and kept them in the kitchen especially for us. It was ironic really, as I didn't eat meat, but all the same, the gesture was very touching.

The team at The Meat Co. was so obliging that on my birthday they said they would cook me whatever I liked, even if it was not on the menu.

"Anything you want," Hannan, our waiter, said. "The chef wants you to have whatever you wish for tonight."

And with that, he produced a bottle of champagne as a gift from the manager, and a cake followed later at the end of the meal. Everyone in the restaurant was smiling and singing. I will never forget these beautiful souls who made our Thursday evenings so special. There wasn't a lot to do in Bahrain, so this made our stay there worthwhile.

That particular night, though, the atmosphere was a little different. Aside from the constant coughing, Rick seemed uneasy and on edge. He was certainly not enjoying his food with the usual gusto.

"Food keeps getting stuck," he said apologetically.

"What do you mean?" I asked. "Maybe the meat is a bit chewy?"

SAOIRSE BROWN

"I dunno," he said with a shrug. "I just can't seem to swallow properly. It's happened a couple of times now. I had a complete coughing fit when I was out with the blokes the other night."

"Maybe something just got stuck," I said.

It didn't seem like anything to be alarmed about. All the same, after seeing a worried look flit across Rick's face, I decided it might be worth checking out.

"Shall I book you in to see the docs?"

"Nah," Rick said dismissively.

He'd always hated making a fuss. He'd hated visiting doctors for as long as I could remember. His entire medical philosophy was based around the maxim of saying nothing and it'll probably just clear up itself.

"Besides, there is way too much to get done before we swan off to Europe for a couple of months," he said with an air that definitely signaled the conversation was closed.

"What about when we get to the UK then?" I suggested. "It'll only take a few minutes to check you out."

Rick mumbled something that sounded like, "If you have to," as he left the table. He really, really didn't want to talk about it.

So, I'd taken matters in my own hands and booked the appointment at Ashtead Hospital near our house in Leatherhead, Surrey. We'd bought the four-bedroom detached house a few years earlier after many years of not owning a house in the UK. With the kids now at a boarding school—Cranbrook School in Kent, which wasn't too far away—it made sense to have a permanent base here because we'd inevitably be spending more time in the UK. I'd fully expected a couple of tests, a charming lecture about taking care of yourself and perhaps a few tablets to clear up some sort of infection.

Never for one moment did I expect: *It doesn't look good.*

That weekend, after the shock of the hospital visit, I did my best to hide my worries from Rick and the children. As usual, we had a packed schedule of social events. We came to England so rarely that everyone was always so keen to see us. Earlier, I'd spent weeks juggling our diary to try to make sure we spent time with all our close friends. On Saturday, we were due to be at the golf club for lunch. The plan was that the male side of the friendship group would stay on for a round afterward, while the ladies would spend time at our house that afternoon.

God knows how I made it through the lunch. I kept glancing anxiously over at Rick, checking for signs of stress or distress, but he seemed perfectly calm and composed. I was a wreck, though. I barely heard anything anyone said, and even when I did, I couldn't follow the thread of the conversation. It all just felt so surreal. Why on earth were we sitting outside in the sunshine sipping rosé when it felt like my life was being snatched away from me?

It doesn't look good.

By the time I climbed into the car for the journey back to Leatherhead, I was struggling to know where I was.

"Are you okay?" my good friend Karen asked gently. She'd just climbed into the passenger seat. "I've been chatting away, but I don't think you heard a word."

That was enough of a trigger to open the floodgates. Tears poured down my cheeks, and in a few seconds, I was sobbing uncontrollably, my breath coming in deep, gasping rasps.

"It's Rick," I managed to stammer between sobs. "The doctor says it doesn't look good. They've done all these tests. We just don't know."

Karen gave me a hug. I clung to her like a drowning woman.

When I eventually calmed down enough to talk, I told my friend what had been going on. She listened in silence, barely moving as I spoke. Her eyes were wide with concern.

"I'm sure it is nothing," she said again and again as I finished.

"We just don't know, though," I said.

"You've got to think the best," Karen said. "Even if it is something, there is loads that can be done these days. Come on, let's get you home."

Karen looked after me through the afternoon, making me cup of tea after cup of tea in that peculiarly British way, as though a warm drink could somehow take away the pain and anguish I felt. I appreciated what she was doing, but I just yearned for the weekend to end. I just wanted to know. The doctor had asked us to return first thing on Monday, but that felt like a million years away.

I'd managed to stop crying by the time Rick returned. It was impossible to pretend, though. He took one look at my blotchy face and immediately knew what was going on. The second I saw that he knew I had been crying, I started all over again.

"I am so sorry," I whispered. "I'm just so worried."

Rick took me in his arms and held me tight. For a while neither of us said anything. We just held onto each other, finding comfort in the familiar warmth and closeness of our bodies.

"Don't worry. Come on, it's nothing," he said at last, stepping back and looking into my eyes. "Let's just enjoy the weekend together and forget about it for now."

I nodded as he tenderly brushed some hair away from my eyes.

"You dragged me over here, so the least you can do is enjoy it." He smiled.

Somehow—I'll never know how—we managed to get through the rest of the weekend without mentioning the upcoming appointment again. But not mentioning it was not the same as not thinking about it. I thought about what might happen on Monday morning every second as the weekend crawled by at a snail's pace. It easily felt like the longest weekend of my life. I know it was the same for Rick, who woke up frequently during each night, obviously concerned about what was to come after the weekend.

On Monday morning, we were back in the clinical white surrounds of the doctor's office. Even as we were shown in I noticed the short, dark-haired doctor seemed very different from the last time we'd met. That previous Friday, which felt a world away now, he'd started off by asking how we were and what we felt about coming back to the British weather. This time, though, he stayed silent as we took our seats. He was holding a file of paperwork in his right hand and a pen in the other. A nurse was sitting in one corner of the room, as though ready to take notes.

I wondered how bad it could actually be. Things seemed very serious now. It wasn't long before we were to find out. The words that would come out of the doctor's mouth would stay with me forever.

"As explained on Friday, your symptoms and the results of the tests we were able to see didn't look good," he began briskly, jumping right into it.

I caught my breath but forced myself to listen to every word. I need to know what we were dealing with.

"The results have come back, and you have esophageal cancer," he said, looking straight at Rick.

Instinctively, I reached over and took my husband's hand. His palm was ice cold but moist with sweat.

"Stage four," continued the doctor.

"Stage four?" I repeated. I had no idea what that even meant. I had never had to deal with cancer before.

The doctor explained each stage to us. I kept drifting in and out of listening to the doctor and then my own thoughts.

Then he said: "Statistically, most patients don't survive longer than twelve months when diagnosed at this stage."

I stared at the doctor uncomprehendingly. Twelve months? Rick was just forty-six years old. Sure, he had been a little tired lately, and there was the thing with the food ... but cancer? Terminal cancer?

There had to be a mistake.

"We need to get you booked in with an oncologist at the Royal Marsden as soon as possible and get you started on chemotherapy straight away. We will try and manage it best we can."

What do you do with that information? What does anyone do when they are told they have months to live or that their husband is suffering from untreatable cancer? I knew I should ask lots of questions. There was so much I needed to know, but I couldn't think. It was impossible. It had all been so quick. How do you hear something like that and then function? Well, you don't.

Chapter 2

▬ ▬ ▬ ▬ ▬ ▬ ▬ ▬ ▬ ▬ ▬ ▬ ▬

THE ROLLER COASTER OF TREATMENT

I don't know how we got through the days that followed the diagnosis. There seemed to be so much to do or talk about, and yet nothing seemed to work as it should—certainly not my brain anyhow. I just couldn't think properly. Nothing made sense.

I would watch neighbors driving off to work or listen to people discussing the holidays they were planning, all the while wondering how this could all be happening. I kept thinking, *How on earth are things still moving when our lives are standing still? Why has the world not stopped?* It was just us, suspended in time.

Rick seemed shocked by the diagnosis, but not as shocked as I was. I wasn't sure what he had taken in or if, in fact, he had taken it in at all. What made it all the worse was he was still doing his best to hide the horror and grief from me and the children. He tried to be as upbeat as he possibly could.

"It'll be all right, treasure," he'd say.

How?

Of course, at the same time as struggling to digest the information, we also needed to find a way to explain the unexplainable to other people. Naturally, I shouldered most of this task. The calls took on an eerily familiar format. A cheery "How are you?" greeting from the family member or friend on the other end of the phone, followed by me telling them they needed to brace themselves for some terrible news. I'd deliver the blow, which would invariably be met by a shocked silence, then tears, and then a flood of questions about the plan for treatment. Everyone seemed to know someone who had beaten cancer or who had done this that or the other to prolong their diagnosis. The messages were all one of hope, telling us to persevere.

But no one could quite bring themselves to say: It'll be okay. Because it wouldn't be.

It doesn't look good.

Rick took on the task of calling his employer back in Abu Dhabi. They were understanding and told him to take all the time he needed. They didn't discuss the fact that it was highly likely he would never return to work. They didn't have to. That was a conversation for another day.

The worst thing of all was telling Rick's mother. I had insisted we would need to drive up north to Todmorden in West Yorkshire to tell her. This wasn't something she needed to hear over the phone. When we gently broke the news, she looked as I imagined I did upon hearing the diagnosis: shocked, confused, and most probably in denial about what she had just heard.

After the consultation with the oncologist, and Rick agreeing to the treatment plan that was offered, the treatment began almost immediately. Rick was back in the hospital beginning his first course of chemotherapy just days after the diagnosis. I'd taken it upon myself to read everything I could about the treatment and the potential progress of the disease itself, but Rick closed himself off from it. He stoically turned up to his appointments, did what he was required to do, but never really spoke about it in any depth. Initially, I would try and talk to him about it, but he didn't seem to dwell on it too much, and he would swiftly guide the conversation to another topic. After a while, I didn't push the point. He had to deal with things in his own way. Throughout it all—and I had no idea how—he kept his positive demeanor.

"It'll be fine," he'd smile, "as long as you'll still love me as a bald man."

I knew he was only half joking about this. Rick loved his hair—and rightly so. It was beautiful. When we first met, he had long, thick, dark hair that he spent more time drying and messing around with than I did mine. His hair had just a hint of waviness, and he would make sure to stand in front of the mirror, drying it carefully to make quite sure the waves were completely straightened out. He'd only cut it short when he'd started working in the office because he felt it was more in keeping with his managerial role and made him more presentable. Therefore, he'd had short hair for the past few years. Now, though, he was concerned that he would lose it all thanks to the chemo.

I knew from my research that the drug he'd be using wasn't one that normally meant hair loss, and the doctor also tried to put Rick at ease about this, but all the same it worried him a lot.

As expected, the chemo was awful. Each treatment would leave him feeling sick and tired for days afterward. He looked tired and didn't want to go anywhere, preferring to stay at home. He began to eat a lot less due to the sickness, coupled with the struggle of swallowing anything, and the weight began to drop from his previously well-honed frame. I hated seeing my formerly fit, healthy, and vibrant husband reduced to a shell of his former self. I'd often catch him staring in the mirror to check on his hair to see if it was falling out. It did become thinner, but he didn't look to be losing much, which was a relief, albeit a small one.

I went with Rick on each trip to the hospital. I tried to give him a word of encouragement and put him at ease as he recoiled each time we walked through the sliding doors, but it was heartbreaking. Just the smell of the hospital made him feel nauseous. It was the signal that the after-chemo sickness was just moments away.

There were many hours spent waiting in uncomfortable reception areas. Waiting for our turn. Waiting for his treatment. Waiting to see a doctor or consultant. Over time, I saw many of the same faces. I noticed the friends and relatives all shared the same desperate look of hopelessness. It was probably because I knew exactly how they were all feeling that I struck up conversations with many of my fellow waiters. Soon, I began to speak to the patients too.

I learned that Rick and I were comparatively lucky. Our home was just ten minutes down the road from the Royal Marsden, Sutton. The others in the waiting room frequently traveled miles for their treatments. Many would either drive back home the same day or be forced to book into nearby accommodation because they were too unwell to travel.

Despite the terrible circumstances the overwhelming shared emotion of that group was of hope. It was remarkable how positive they all were too. I couldn't help admiring them all for that. It could have been very easy to be angry with the world, but patients with that mind-set were easily in the minority.

It saddened me to see that some patients arrived alone for treatment. There was one elderly woman in particular in this group who stood out. When we got talking, I discovered she was ninety-three years old. She told me that her husband had passed away many years before, and they hadn't had any children.

"Didn't you want any?" I asked her, thinking how much I loved my own children. I couldn't imagine getting through something like this without their love and support.

"It just never ever happened," she said with a shrug. "Neither of us was particularly bothered about it. We just had each other and enjoyed life together."

As we gradually got to know each other, I became emboldened enough to ask whether there was anyone who could accompany her on her trips to the hospital.

"Oh no, dear, but don't worry about me." She smiled. "I speak to my neighbor occasionally, but I really don't need anyone's help."

"What about getting in touch with Age Concern?" I pressed. "Maybe get a befriender who could take you out once in a while and offer you some company, bring you to the hospital and sit with you?"

The lovely old lady brushed aside the idea and said she was very content just as she was. All the same, it worried me. I knew how grueling the treatments were and didn't think anyone should go through something like that alone.

It didn't help that there seemed to be a constant drip, drip, drip effect of bad news. Being immersed in the waiting room community meant I was constantly aware when someone's prognosis worsened. There certainly rarely seemed to be any good news. Sure enough, after an early round of tests, we discovered that the cancer had spread to Rick's liver, shoulder, and spine.

It was another big shock but, oddly, not as crippling as the initial one. Rick certainly seemed to have gotten in his stride by now.

"It's still just cancer," he said, smiling at me. "I've just got to put more energy into beating it."

Beating it? What a wonderful idea to think that we could defy all odds and beat it. It was so much easier to think about it in this way, though. The other side of this thinking was just too enormous to contemplate. If we discussed timescales at all, it was all about confounding the doctor's predictions.

"If I can make it to five years, I'll be happy," Rick would say. "That's what I am focusing on. Then, who knows?"

Me? I'd just take every second of time I could get. I couldn't imagine life without Rick. He was still relentlessly upbeat, but it was easy to see the toll this disease was taking on him. When he was well enough, he'd distract himself by playing his guitar and listening to music, which had long been his way to relax. The veneer of "being okay" was paper thin, though, as he seemed to be doing everything he could to blank out the enormity of it all. In fact, he was so keen to try and forget about hospital appointments and what was next in the barrage of tests that constantly seemed to be required, he handed over that side of it to me. I would deal with the medical appointments and just let him know where we needed to be and when. If the hospital called, he would just say: "Can you speak to my wife please?"

There would be good days when we would venture out to visit friends or simply try to get out and do something different. Of course, we had to take it day by day. On one of the good days, Rick was able to take up an invitation to spend a day on the track at Brands Hatch. Aston Martin would book a day there for anyone who wished to take his or her car for a spin around a racetrack. Fortunately, Rick was well enough to go. We both knew that the drive along the German Autobahn we'd talked about a few months earlier wasn't going to happen now. This was the next best thing.

We were allowed to bring two guests, so our friends Karen and David came along. I even had a go, not driving, though, and certainly not being driven by Rick. There was no way I was going to get into any car being driven around a racetrack by my husband. I chose a professional driver, although as he accelerated around the track at breakneck speed, I was not sure that was a good idea either. Remarkably, the driver chatted away so calmly as he negotiated hairpin bends he could just as easily have been hanging out his washing.

"What have you got planned for the weekend?" he said, glancing over at me and smiling. "Anything nice?"

Eyes on the road. Eyes on the road, I repeated inside my head, my hands gripping the seat below me so hard my fingers hurt. I'll admit it now: the F-word came out a few times, particularly on the sharp bends where I'm sure we were on only two wheels for a brief period. I'd apologize profusely for my language when we hit the straights and do my best to answer his question. Then, as soon as we swerved into the next bend, the F-word would pop out again. Once again, I would apologize as soon as we straightened up. The entire track run continued in this manner. Sheer terror and bad language notwithstanding, it was lovely to relax for a while after all we had been through. It was hard to truly get away from the enormity of what Rick and I faced, but days like that were very special. Sadly, they were becoming fewer and further in between.

A few months after the treatment started we were called in to see Rick's consultant. We didn't say it, but we both approached the appointment with quite a bit of trepidation. Discussions like this were always times to deliver good or bad news. Lately, there had been a lot more of the latter.

We shuffled into the doctor's office and sat down opposite him. I did my best to read the doctor's face but couldn't quite get a handle on it.

"I have good news," he said at last. He hadn't exactly broken into a grin, but he looked markedly more upbeat than he had at other appointments. "The condition of the liver has improved. There are only a couple of small spots left remaining."

Rick and I exchanged glances, and I could see his eyes shining. For a moment, he looked like the Rick I knew from months earlier. Those were the days before we'd given a second thought to what might be around the corner.

"We're not out of the woods," the doctor continued. "The cancer is still in the esophagus and bone; however, given how successful the first round of treatment has been, we are very hopeful that with some radiotherapy, we will be able to shrink some more."

It was all we needed to hear. For a second, it felt like a Christmas, birthday, and wedding day all rolled into one. In one second, the doctor had given us the biggest gift of them all: hope. Hope that this sentence Rick had been given could be prolonged.

The doctor smiled as I hugged Rick.

"I really can't believe how well you look," the doctor expressed to Rick. "I have honestly never seen anyone with your condition look quite so well. This all bodes well."

I listened carefully as the doctor began to outline the next stage of treatment. Rick shifted in his chair uncomfortably. He never liked to hear the detail. He was much more of a let's-get-on-with-it type of person. When the doctor said the treatment wouldn't begin for a fortnight, I suddenly had an idea.

"Do you think we could go away? You know, take a break somewhere abroad?"

I glanced over to Rick, who was looking a bit surprised.

"Come on," I smiled, squeezing his leg. "It's been a tough few months, and you could do with a holiday."

"Would that be okay from your point of view?" I said, turning to face the doctor.

"Sure, it's a good idea. Rest up and gather your strength. Enjoy some time away from the hospital."

After we left the hospital, it took me a few days to persuade Rick that this was a good idea. He needed to get away, experience some different scenery, and immerse himself into something else for a while. Once I convinced him that this was the thing to do, he seemed quite excited by the prospect. Now we just had to decide where.

The idea we kept coming back to was Italy, which was somewhere we'd both wanted to go for a while. My long-held dream was to go there via the Orient Express, but Rick flat out refused that one. He'd always hated dressing up. He'd have lived his entire life in tracksuit trousers if I had let him. It was almost impossible to get him into a suit. He'd once even turned down the opportunity to go to the premiere of a James Bond movie because of it. We had been offered tickets because we owned an Aston Martin, and it promised to be an achingly glam affair, but he flatly refused because he didn't want to wear black tie! I knew the chances of me getting him into one for a trip across Europe on the oh-so-refined Orient Express were nonexistent, and he told me as much.

It wasn't that Rick was some sort of antihero or reverse snob. He'd always hated anything that smacked of shallow or inauthentic behavior. He hated the idea that people judge others on what they wear. Just one year earlier (or a million years ago in cancer time) when we'd bought the Aston Martin, the staff had eyed us very suspiciously when we'd gone to the salesroom. We both knew they were thinking we were just dreamers window-shopping. Then Rick had taken them by surprise by walking up to the salesman and saying: "I'd like to buy that one." That was a great moment for Rick, fulfilling his life ambition and deservedly so after all the hard work he'd put in over the years. It also confirmed his view that most people are innate snobs who are too quick to judge a person by the cut of his or her jib.

Rick agreed to a tour of Florence, Venice, and Pisa, but on conventional transport only. I didn't mind. It was just nice for us to have some time away, enjoy one another's company, and relax. Italy is beautiful and never more so than in late winter. The weather was cold but crisp, fresh, and sunny. We wrapped up warm, spending our time doing very little but just loving being together. If Rick was up to it, we took in the sights, but when he felt tired, we were just as happy to sit in a coffee shop people-watching.

For a while, we were so immersed in each other and our surroundings we almost forgot what faced us when we got home. Almost. Like the cancer that was eating away at my husband, the thought of what he had to shortly go through, never quite went away.

Sure enough, before we knew it, we were back in the UK having more tests and starting the new therapy. He needed blood tests to make sure he was fit to start chemo again and various scans and ultrasounds to chart the progress of the cancer.

The next couple of months were even more difficult for Rick than the initial bouts of chemo. After the radiotherapy began, he had a couple of operations to fit stents that would open up the esophagus, both of which failed. Every day we seemed to wake up to a new disappointment, but we just had to keep plowing on with the hope that the next run of chemotherapy and the radiotherapy running alongside it would make an impact. Meanwhile, Rick was in almost constant discomfort. It broke my heart to see him this way.

In the back of our minds, we were still clinging onto hope. Now that we'd articulated the idea of five years (or maybe even beyond!), we'd somehow manage to get through each day believing the next big push would see us through. Keep believing: *it's gonna be okay.*

After a couple more months, we were called in to see the consultant again. This time, we were more apprehensive than ever. In our hearts, we prayed it was another good-news conversation, but somehow, we both sensed it wasn't.

We were right.

The next batch of tests answered our worst fears. The cancer had come back to the liver, and this time more aggressively than ever.

"I'm afraid there is a little more we can do," the doctor said quietly after going over the recent test results and showing us the scans. "Chemotherapy wouldn't help the disease anymore."

The silence stretched between us for a few seconds as we drank in the enormity of the disappointment.

"We can do another run of chemotherapy if you would like, but I am of the opinion it will make little to no difference," the doctor said, repeating the message in a slightly different way, perhaps to ensure we understood.

I saw Rick nod slowly as he processed what was being said.

"Alternatively," the doctor continued, "you may like to consider taking part in a clinical trial."

I knew all about these trials. I'd read all about them in my many late nights of scrolling through the internet, trying to find something, anything that might help us. I hadn't been keen when I had read about them and wasn't keen now. I didn't think there was much chance at all it would help. It could even make things worse. I also hated the idea of my husband being a guinea pig.

At the end of the day, though, it was entirely Rick's decision.

"Tell me about the trial," I heard my husband say as he fixed his full attention on the doctor.

After the doctor explained about the aims and extent of the trial, Rick agreed to go away and think about it. I suspected that Rick had already made up his mind, but because he knew I wasn't keen, he was making a show of weighing it up carefully.

We had a fortnight to decide whether to go ahead, and under my encouragement, we took a brief trip back to Abu Dhabi. It was

March 2016, and Rick had been away from work for nine months. I knew he was keen to catch up with his friends and work colleagues. He'd really missed his job and the banter he had with everyone he had in the office and on the rigs.

Sadly, we couldn't re-create the magic of our recent trip to Italy. Rick had begun to feel quite unwell even before we had landed, and even the prospect of a swim in the hotel pool could only encourage him outside on a few occasions. Toward the end of the week he preferred to stay in the hotel room reading, only leaving the room to meet up with friends over a coffee, and we went out for dinner just the once. By this stage, Rick's ability to eat anything solid was becoming more and more difficult, so he stuck to softer foods.

It was nice to see him enjoying being back with his friends and having a laugh like the old days, but the time like this was tragically brief. It broke my heart as I thought back to weekends in years gone by. Typically, our Abu Dhabi mates would meet up for a brunch and socialize long into the night. The oil and gas industry is a twenty-four-hour operation and the guys were always kept busy, so this was their way of relaxing after a hard week at work. They worked and played hard, enjoying being in one another's company. I know Rick enjoyed the brief glimpse back into his old life, but he was more than relieved to go home when the time came. The trip had exhausted what little reserve of strength he had left.

As soon as we arrived back, we received the news that early results from the clinical trial looked promising.

"Let's do this," he said to me after we heard. "Maybe it'll be positive for me too."

Of course, I agreed straight away. I had to hope that this would work for Rick. Right then, hope was all we had to cling to.

Chapter 3

— — — — — — — — — — — — —

NO WORDS

Rick and I had always been chalk and cheese. He was a gregarious, open, life and soul of the party, while I preferred the company of a handful of very close friends. He'd always be looking for the next crazy adventure, while I wanted to get things done. Although he was always desperate to please me, he was always in too much of a rush to do anything practical like fixing a leak or moving furniture. If I ever wanted anything done, he'd tell me to write it down and make him a list. Woe betide me if I later mentioned anything that hadn't been on the list! He'd go nuts. A long rant would ensue, which basically centered around the fact that he had allocated a certain amount of time for these chores and had his own stuff to get on with. It used to drive me crazy.

To-do lists notwithstanding, we rarely argued. In fact, we got on so well our friends often remarked on our seemingly model marriage. I guess opposites attract. I think the secret was that we always talked. We may not have always agreed, but almost everything was up for discussion.

The only subject Rick had long steered clear from, even before he was sick, was death. Anything that even smacked of the end of our days, or the afterlife, was usually quickly shut down with a dismissive swipe of his hand or a rapid change of subject. If he said anything at all, it was to loudly denounce all forms of an afterlife as a "complete load of rubbish." When our dog Clay had died a few years earlier, he had come back to me in spirit a couple of days after his passing to let me know he was okay. When I mentioned this to Rick, he would have none of it.

"There's no such thing as the afterlife," he'd said. "When you are gone, you are gone."

I wonder if the idea had played on his mind, because not long after we had this talk about Clay, we had a very strange conversation. We were on one of our annual trips to England, and as usual, it had been a huge struggle to get Rick to come back. All the usual moans and groans about the weather had been played out, and after weeks of protests, he had finally relented. I think what may have swung it was I promised to take him to the Toby's Carvery near our home in Surrey. It all goes to show that the old saying about the way to a man's heart being through his stomach is entirely true. It was almost impossible to get a decent roast dinner in the United Arab Emirates.

So, there we were, sitting with our roast dinners, complete with all the trimmings and a nice glass of wine, when I noticed that Rick had not said a word for ages. He had what could only be described as a thousand-yard stare as he slowly chewed his food and was clearly completely lost in thought.

I left him to it for a long while. We'd known each long enough to be comfortable with each other's silence. I assumed that he was worrying about how things were going in the office. He always worked so hard and had such a lot on his plate that he found it very difficult to switch off.

"Are you thinking about work?" I asked gently as we finished our meals.

Rick paused and looked at me. He looked like he was weighing up what to say.

"No, I'm just looking around at all of these old people, and I have decided that I don't want to get old," he said at last.

His response caught me completely off guard. I never expected him to say something like that. Deciding to go with it, I glanced around us. Rick was right. The majority of the customers in the carvery must have been older than sixty-five, many considerably older. It stood out all the more after our lengthy time in the Middle East where it is rare to see many of the older generation out and about. We'd been away for so many years, it often felt like the UK was the foreign land to us.

"It's all relative, you know," I laughed. "These people don't think they are old, just like you don't feel like you are old at the ripe old age of forty-two. I bet people in their twenties look at us and thing we're old and past it, though.

"Why did you bring it up? You don't feel old, do you?"

I noticed Rick wasn't smiling back. Whatever it was that was bothering him was serious. I stayed silent to give him space to articulate his thoughts.

"No, I don't feel old now," he said slowly. "I've just made some decisions about what we are going to do when we do get older. You know, when we get to a point of not being able to look after ourselves and start being a burden to the kids."

I stared back at him. I was almost scared to hear what he was about to say.

"We are going to rent a chalet somewhere where there is plenty of snow," he went on. "We will walk outside, sit down in the snow, and let the cold take us. Hypothermia kicks in, you become unconscious, and then you die. You feel nothing. That's what we will do."

For a few moments, the silence grew between us. Rick stared at me, as though he was trying to gauge my reaction. A thousand thoughts flooded into my head as I struggled to understand why my husband was saying something like this now. I'm not sure I could compute any of it, so I resorted to the easiest possible response: I made a joke out of it.

"My word, that's a bit heavy," I giggled. "I only came out for Sunday lunch. I didn't expect to be included in a suicide pact!"

Fortunately, Rick laughed too, and the spell, or whatever it was that induced that strange conversation, was broken. Well, almost broken. Before he dropped the conversation, Rick had one more thing to say.

"Just promise me one thing," he said, looking deep into my eyes. "Just say you will help me die with dignity if I am ever unable to live a functioning life."

"I promise," I said without hesitation. I was serious too.

"If for any reason it isn't possible to take you to Switzerland, or wherever it is we need to go, if I had to help you die," I said, and then, more quietly, I added, "I would do whatever I needed to do, without question."

"And I would do the same," he said.

The conversation was over as quickly and unexpectedly as it began. We never spoke of it again. Not even when Rick was first diagnosed.

As Rick's disease worsened, I did think of what we'd promised that day. Obviously, I didn't raise it with Rick, but I wondered how much pain was too much. I also wondered if I would ever have been able to keep my promise. Now that it could be a reality, I just couldn't see how it was possible to help my husband die. I loved him so much I'd have taken every spare second I could have with him, however sick he got. The thought of cutting it short, even by a matter of hours, just didn't seem right. I couldn't bear to lose him.

However, as much as I didn't want to think about what might be, it was clear Rick was growing weaker by the day now. The once-prized Aston Martin, which sat outside on the drive, forgotten and undriven, symbolized everything that was happening. This vehicle, which had once given Rick so much joy, was now just a useless carcass of fiberglass and metal. Once he would have made any excuse to take her for a spin. He'd even offer to do the food shopping in it, which was unheard of. Yet, these days he couldn't even summon up the energy to go outside, let alone take it for a spin.

Saoirse Brown

The man I married who loved life so much, grasping every thrill and opportunity with both hands, was fading before my eyes.

I still took my regular walk with our dog Maisy. I barely slept any more, going to bed late and rising early, but relied on my time outside in the early hours to compose myself before the day ahead. I'd get up at five o'clock in the morning and slip out quietly while Rick slept. I enjoyed the quietness and serenity of my early morning walks, which I believed always fed my soul. It was the best time of day to enjoy all that nature had to offer. Sometimes I would just stand still, drinking it all in, listening to the birds singing, watching wild animals scurrying about their day, and, if I was lucky, watching deer galloping majestically past. It was always my time to reflect, connect, and be at one with nature. It was a perfect moment to give me the sanity I so needed then and the time to breathe.

As the days went on, my walks became shorter and shorter. I felt the urge to rush back to make sure Rick was okay. I didn't want him to wake up and try to struggle to get out of bed or find something he needed. By now, he had become a lot weaker and welcomed my offer of help to shower and dress. I'd help him downstairs, prepare his drinks, and give him his medication. He was barely eating anything at all now, so breakfast wasn't an issue. In fact, solid food of any sort was not an issue. The hospital had prescribed him some high-calorie shakes, but he loathed what he said was the slightly chemical flavor they seemed to have. I prepared his preferred variety.

For a while, I was constantly on edge that he wasn't eating enough, but after doing a little research online, I came to the conclusion that trying to make him eat when he really didn't want to would just result in unnecessary stress for us both. I backed off after that, although I made sure to ask regularly if he fancied anything to eat. The answer was always no, though, so I left it at that. As long as Rick was drinking his shakes and some water, that was enough.

It broke my heart that everything Rick had once enjoyed in life—whether it was rocking out on his guitar; playing golf; or drinking, eating, and socializing—meant nothing to him now. All his fight and vigor seemed to have ebbed away, and that was difficult to watch. He'd also stopped taking phone calls from friends who would call constantly for updates or just to say hello.

"Not now," Rick would say when I tried to pass on the calls. "I'm too tired."

I tried and tried to convince him to speak to them. Many of these people had been friends for decades and were naturally desperate to speak to him or help in any way they could, but he just couldn't face it. I had no choice but to respect this choice.

"I'm really sorry, but he doesn't wish to talk. He's too tired," I'd tell well-wisher after well-wisher. They were always polite to me as I did my best to update them on Rick's progress, but I could tell they would have much preferred to talk to the man himself.

Even celebrating his forty-seventh birthday was a quiet affair, with just a handful of family members. I had a birthday cake made in the shape of his favorite guitar, which put a smile on his face, but he didn't wish to go out and make a big deal out of the occasion.

The first round of clinical trials had been completed, and he had had more scans and blood tests to check if there had been any improvement. As the day approached to visit the hospital to get the results from the doctor, the tension became almost unbearable. Neither of us felt prepared for any bad news, but we both knew that things were not looking good.

When the actual day came, Rick seemed weaker than ever. He needed assistance every step of the way, and everything needed to be done in stages. Get out of bed … rest. Shower … rest. Get dressed … rest. Come downstairs … rest. Part of it was that, understandably, Rick was in no real hurry to get to the hospital, but a great deal of the problem was he no longer had the energy to do much of anything. Fortunately, the staff at the Royal Marsden were always really good if we were late, which hadn't been often since we'd started treatment. They understood that sometimes it just couldn't be helped. We'd always started getting ready early to make sure of that, but this time it seemed to take longer than ever.

SAOIRSE BROWN

The drive over the Epsom Downs had always been one we enjoyed. On a clear day, you could see London in the distance. Some evenings, when Rick just fancied getting out for some fresh air but didn't want to do much, we would sit on the Downs and look at the lights of London. On that day, though, we barely noticed the beauty around us. Deep down, we both knew that, this time, the visit to the hospital would be different.

As we arrived at the hospital, I braced myself for Rick's customary wince as the sliding doors eased open. He hated that smell with all his being. The sharp, sour odor of disinfectant seemed to sum up all his pain and misery in one package. We used the children's ward entrance, as we often did, because it was more accessible. It was a difficult journey, though, seeing the sick young children, many with visible hair loss as they sat in wheelchairs with feeding tubes attached. I couldn't comprehend how the parents of these children must have been feeling.

Rick would often relax a little once we got talking with the staff. There were many familiar faces to us now, and they were all amazing—so kind and giving. Despite the hardship they saw each day, they always had smiles on their faces and an apparently never-ending stream of jokes to give the patients a laugh. Rick even had a favorite nurse he would always insist on seeing when there was any requirement to draw his blood. This particular lady was quick and always got it right, with no pain and no bruising. He hated needles, always had, so his face would drop if she wasn't around for him. In fact, despite his lack of energy, he would try to hunt her down, going from room to room to find where she was. He was adamant that she and no one else be the one to take his blood.

We'd spent so much time at that hospital, Rick became almost comfortable and at home there once he got over the hurdle of getting through those doors and ignoring the evocative smells—at least as comfortable and at home as it is possible to be under the circumstance. He certainly had no qualms about asking for what he needed. He hated being in the crowded room for chemotherapy.

If he saw the room filling up, he would request the end room—it was always quiet in there. The nurses always willingly opened the end room up for him if there was a bigger demand for treatment on that day.

We were asked to wait in the busy waiting room and took our seats, as we had done so many times before. As always, I looked at the other people seated anxiously around us. No doubt, nearly everyone there was waiting for a test result, wondering which way their lives were going to go. As I knew oh so well, it's an awful situation to be in. Yet, it doesn't matter how much you want it to go away—how much you want things to rewind—it is as it is. This is the hand you've been dealt.

We were waiting for the tall, slim doctor with the receding hairline to arrive. You'd never know from his demeanor whether it was to be good news or bad news. He always looked serious either way. The only clue would be when a Macmillan nurse was invited in to the consultation. Then you knew it was going to be bad.

"Richard Howorth?"

It was the tall, slim doctor. He was alone.

I helped Rick to his feet, and we slowly walked toward the consulting room as the doctor stood aside to let us walk in first.

Rick and I both saw her at virtually the same moment. A Macmillan nurse, sitting in the chair beside the doctor's desk. She was smiling warmly, her hands clasped together on her lap.

So this was it.

My heart fell to the pit of my stomach.

It was bad news. The worst.

The doctor began with some small talk. Weather. Traffic. Busy day. It was all the same. He could have recited the alphabet. We both responded politely. Rick even managed a couple of weak jokes. But we just wanted the doctor to get on with it.

Or maybe it was better he never got started. That way, we'd be suspended in time for ever, and nothing bad could happen.

Before I knew it, small talk was over.

Saoirse Brown

"I'm very sorry, but you'll deteriorate markedly over the next couple of weeks," the doctor said, looking at Rick steadily.

I wondered if I had heard correctly. *Deteriorate? Was that a euphemism for the fact that Rick was not going to be with us much longer?* I had the strangest sensation—like I had stepped away from myself and was observing from afar. This wasn't really happening. It couldn't be.

Strangely, it was Rick who found the power to respond, even though God knows he must have been as stunned as I was.

"So, when shall I come and see you again?" he said.

The trace of a frown flitted past the doctor's brow, and he shifted slightly in his chair.

"I'm sorry. There is no need for you to come back and see me. You will deteriorate rapidly within the next couple of weeks," the doctor repeated with emphasis.

It was Rick's turn to frown slightly. Why wasn't the doctor answering his question?

"So, when shall I come and see you again?" Rick said again.

The doctor paused and glanced over to the Macmillan nurse, as if for reassurance.

"There is no need to come back. There is nothing more we can do."

My head began to spin. I felt my heart race and my stomach churn. I glanced over at Rick who looked shattered, a crumpled shell of himself. A couple of weeks? Was that all we had? How could that possibly be? I wanted to jump to my feet and run out of the room, or scream and shout, or shake the doctor and tell him he had made a mistake, or demand a second opinion. I knew all of that was crazy and futile. I had to support Rick.

Say something, I shouted inwardly. *Anything!*

"Is the cancer any better in the liver? Is it better than before?" I asked.

Really? Did you not just hear what the doctor just said? Why would you ask such a ridiculous question?

To his credit, the doctor did remark on the daftness of my question.

"There really is nothing more that can be done, so I didn't take the time to compare scans," he said gently.

The Macmillan nurse started to offer words of comfort, but I didn't hear any of them. I knew she was only doing her job, which I am sure she was very good at, but I just didn't want to be there anymore.

"Let's go home," I said, taking Rick's hand.

He nodded, and I helped him to his feet. I could tell he wanted out of there as much as I did. I'm not sure how we made it out of the waiting room. I felt so weak at the knees. I have no idea how Rick managed it. I'd barely made it down the corridor before I needed to sit down. Luckily, we managed to find a tiny side room where I collapsed into a chair and cried like a baby. I wanted so much to be strong for my husband, but I just couldn't do it right at that moment. None of what had been happening over the past few months had felt real, but now it did. The doctor had said it: a couple of weeks left. Now that it had been articulated, it was like a ticking time bomb. I didn't want it. It wasn't for us. I wanted to run away from it as far as I could go. Rick said nothing. He was completely numb. I hoped he would park this news, just like he had done on so many other occasions. It was how he had always coped, and he needed to be able to do that more than ever that day.

Eventually, I stopped crying enough for us to make it to the car park. *Keep it together. Keep it together,* I repeated to myself like a mantra as we headed down the corridors. I had to stay strong for Rick. It was the least I could do.

We were both silent on the drive home. We needed to reflect on what had been said. When we arrived home, it was me who broke the silence. I so desperately needed to know how Rick was feeling.

"Are you okay?" I said, as I switched off the engine.

"I feel the same as I normally do when we leave the hospital," he said, staring ahead.

"I'm talking about the two-week comment that the doctor mentioned," I pressed.

Silence.

"I don't want to think about that now," he said, opening the car door to signal that our conversation was now over.

I knew from a lifetime's experience that it was impossible to get Rick to open up if he didn't want to talk about something. Although we'd always been really close, he'd shut down a conversation stone dead if he hadn't wanted to go there. I couldn't really blame him in this situation or find any fault.

I completely understood that the only way to cope with the news was to withdraw into his own little world and not to share his darkest thoughts, but I yearned to take some of the pain away. It wasn't just a self-preservation thing. Rick was so brave and selfless too. From the day of diagnosis to this terrible day's news, he'd chosen not to put any more stress on us as a family and kept most of his thoughts to himself.

However hard it was for me, it was my duty to let him deal with it his own way. It was the best way I could possibly show my intense love for him. Nevertheless, I hated the feeling of being so helpless and alone. Just as I am sure Rick did.

Arriving home, I realized we had another big hurdle to cross that day. What were we going to tell the children? Rick had never spoken properly to our children about his cancer. Whenever it was mentioned, he had always kept a positive attitude, and he had certainly never made reference to the possibility that he wouldn't beat this cruel disease.

"I'm a survivor, not a statistic," was his mantra whenever the kids asked him about it.

It had been left to me to give the kids small, highly edited updates after each hospital visit. We'd sit and cry together and try to make sense of it all while shielding Rick from our despair as much as we possibly could.

Of course, now we needed to have the serious conversation he'd been avoiding for months. His illness could no longer be ignored or made light of. The children had to be told the awful news.

I don't remember much of the rest of that terrible day. I know I told the children, and there were a lot of tears and anguish. I remember the kids wanted to stay in their rooms and were too upset to come downstairs. And Rick ... He just sat in complete silence. I joined him in his vigil, neither of us saying anything.

There were no words.

SAOIRSE BROWN

Chapter 4

I LOVE YOU, TREASURE

The following day there was a strange stillness in the air. The children both chose to go about their day, and I was pleased about that. They needed normality at a time like this. They'd need it even more in the months to come. Because it was warm and sunny, Rick and I had decided to sit outside in the garden. Rick had always enjoyed lying on our long corner sofa while he read his books. It was in the sunniest spot in the garden, surrounded by an aromatic jasmine bush.

Today, when he took up his favorite position once again, there was no book. He didn't even have the strength or interest to turn the pages. He couldn't even enjoy the sunshine, which had long been one of his favorite things. It seemed to irritate him so I placed an umbrella close by to give him full shade.

"I don't want to wait for *it* to happen," he suddenly blurted out.

I caught my breath as I turned to face him. I dreaded what he was going to say next.

"Why can't we go to Dignitas in Switzerland—do something other than sit and wait?" he said.

I suddenly remembered our conversation at the Toby Carvery, what felt like a lifetime ago. I had made a promise.

But now I knew for sure it was a promise I couldn't keep.

"It doesn't have to be like that," I blustered, suddenly becoming very intent on adjusting the shade that was protecting his spot on the sofa. For a moment, I couldn't face looking at Rick. I didn't want to let him down. But I couldn't lose him.

"Try and relax. Have a glass of wine, and play your guitar," I coaxed.

Even as I said it, I felt foolish. *What do you say to that?* It saddened me deeply to see Rick lose all interest in his music. He had spent years teaching himself to play the guitar and had recorded his music on a regular basis. All that had disappeared ages ago, like all his interests, which had become distant memories.

"Maybe," he said quietly.

Then, after a pause, he added: "I just don't want to be in pain and suffering."

Tears began to flow down my cheeks. I realized I had no right to break my promise. My husband, the man I loved and the father to our beautiful children, was asking for my help. I had no right to turn my back on him now because of my own selfish desire to spend longer with him. I knelt down beside the sofa and took his hands in mine.

"I will do what I need to do, Rick," I vowed.

I meant it too. At that moment, I would have done anything he asked.

"Thank you," he said emphatically.

In twenty-four years of being together, I have never heard him say anything with such heartfelt conviction.

"You need to promise me something too," I said.

Rick nodded to show he was listening.

"You know I believe in the afterlife," I began. "I've told you the story about Clay often enough."

Rick rolled his eyes in mock exasperation.

"If it is ever possible, would you please come back to me? I know 100 percent that I have been here before and that there is life after death."

His reply astonished me.

"I think I have also," he said simply and squeezed my hand.

I was so stunned I could barely speak. After years of dismissing my story as silly nonsense, he was finally agreeing with me. I had so many things to say, questions to ask, and I realized that for the first time in weeks, I felt a little hope for the future.

"Not now," he said, trying to draw the conversation to a full stop. "Let's just enjoy this beautiful day together."

"What am I supposed to do without you?" I sobbed as the heady mix of emotions finally gave way.

"You will be okay," he said, his face crumpling as he appeared to fight back the tears. "Spend a couple of months with Karen and David. You will be okay."

With that, he looked away and said, "That's enough of that."

We never spoke of it again.

The weather the following day was just as warm and sunny, which was nice. It meant Rick could lie outside again. A lady from Princess Alice Hospice arrived for a visit. She had visited a few times before to see if Rick would like to talk about anything. Often on these visits I would try and make myself scarce so Rick could ask anything he needed without me being around. More often than not, though, even if the visit involved a doctor's examination, he would ask me to stay.

I was tidying up in a corner of the garden, listening idly to their conversation when Rick said something that stopped me in my tracks.

"How do you die?" he asked.

I could barely breathe as I heard the hospice lady calmly explain how the organs just shut down naturally.

"Are you scared?" I asked. I couldn't help it.

"No," came his matter-of-fact response.

He didn't look scared either.

"I just don't like waiting around for it to happen," he said.

I couldn't believe how calmly he was saying such things. It was as though he was waiting for news on a work contract. I knew he must be feeling scared, but somehow, he was keeping his emotions in check. I had no idea how he was doing it. My emotions were all over the place. One minute I was a complete mess upstairs crying my heart out, and the next I was downstairs taking control of the situation. I realized then I was finding it increasingly difficult to cope and wasn't at all sure I would be ready for what was inevitably to come.

With Rick's permission, I invited my sister Sonia to come and be with us. I needed help, both emotionally and physically. Sonia and Rick had always had a good relationship so he was comfortable with the idea; besides, as always, he was looking out for me.

By this stage, Rick was deteriorating quickly, so I offered to bring our bed downstairs for him to sleep in. He barely had the strength to climb the stairs, so it seemed to make sense. The district nurse suggested bringing a hospital bed when she came to change Rick's morphine driver that afternoon, but I wouldn't hear of it. With the decision made, the furniture was moved around in my husband's guitar room and our bed brought downstairs.

The following day, May 28, 2016, was my birthday. Rick had been out with the kids two weeks prior to buy my card, but by the time the day came, he was too ill to focus properly and had forgotten what day it was. It was late afternoon when he did finally remember, at which point he said an apologetic, "Happy birthday," and gave me my card. I opened my cards, but my presents remained as they were, fully wrapped in all their colorful gaudy paper. I couldn't face doing anything as frivolous as opening gifts. The only present I wanted was to be able to rewind my life—to just keep going back in time so that my lovely husband could be well again.

It had only been a few days since we had left the doctor's office with the worst news imaginable. Rick was, as the doctor had said, deteriorating. He was tired, unfocussed, irritable, and really struggling to settle. It was obvious to anyone who saw him that he was giving up. He was sick of the fight. His body temperature had started to fluctuate badly, and he struggled to cope with this, yet another discomfort in a long line of unbearable discomforts. Any notion of sleeping beside him at night was impossible. I would be in and out of the bed. He'd be cold one minute and in need of being warmed up and then red hot and not wanting me anywhere near to him.

May 29, 2016, was worse. Unusually, Rick got out of bed and wandered around the house, unsettled and highly disorientated. Too hot, too cold, clothes on, clothes off. Whatever I did, I couldn't settle him. I decided to call the district nurse, as I was unsure of what medication to give him that might offer some peace and help him relax. We spoke about his symptoms for a while, and she suggested that I call the on-call doctor. He arrived within the hour and took a few minutes to check Rick over. He then asked if he could have a word with me in private, and Sonia stepped in to sit with Rick.

"His oxygen levels are very low," the doctor said gravely once we were out of earshot. "Do you know what is happening?"

"Yes," I replied.

I surprised myself at how calm I sounded. Somehow, I had gone into some sort of automatic mode. I had no idea of where I got my strength from, but it had appeared when required.

"How long do we have left?" I asked.

"Between twenty-four and forty-eight hours," the doctor said. "I have never known anyone live longer than forty-eight hours at this stage."

The doctor left shortly after delivering the news. I felt numb.

As soon as the door had closed, Sonia met me outside the room. I relayed the conversation to her, and she nodded.

"He knows," she said quietly. "While you were talking to the doc, he turned to me and said, 'It isn't long now, Sonia.'"

My poor Rick. How do you cope knowing something like that?

I took the phone and began calling around Rick's family. It was time for everyone to come and say their goodbyes. Things had changed quite rapidly within a few hours. Rick was now back in bed, barely conscious and hardly talking. Each family member who came to the house took a turn at sitting with him to say everything that they needed to say in private.

The district nurses paid another visit to check Rick over and make sure he was comfortable. They were careful to keep themselves at a discrete distance so that we could have whatever time we had left with Rick alone.

At ten o'clock that night, with most of the visits over, the children asked to spend some time with their dad. Jack went in first, but it was clear he was really struggling. He couldn't bear to see his father so diminished. He kept having to return to the sanctuary of his bedroom to take himself away from the situation.

Sonia, Ellie, and I went to sit with Rick next. By this stage, no one had heard him speak for some hours.

Sensing we were very, very close to the end, I leaned in and whispered in his ear.

"I love you, treasure."

For a second, his eyes flickered open.

"I love you, treasure," he replied weakly.

My heart soared. It was so amazing to hear his voice once more. I didn't think he was able to speak.

With that, Ellie leaned in and said, "I love you, Pops."

"Love you." He smiled falteringly.

I sat and held Rick's hand as the hands of the clock slowly inched forward to one o'clock, the deepest part of the night. Jack stayed in his bedroom, and Ellie decided to try and get some sleep on the sofa in the next room.

As I stared down at my husband, I could barely come to terms with what was happening. Yes, he had undoubtedly lost weight during his illness, but otherwise, he looked well. In this half-light, it was impossible to tell he was sick. Even though his beloved hair had become thinner due to the chemotherapy, he still looked like our Rick.

He seemed like he was asleep, but I still talked to him just in case he could hear me. I told him that we'd had such a wonderful life together and how grateful I was to have met him. I fought back the tears as I said that we had come to a time when I had to tell him that it was okay for him to leave when he was ready.

"We will all be okay," I said. "We all love you very much."

It wasn't long after I had said those words that I witnessed what I assumed to be Rick's spirit leaving his body. His face changed from looking peaceful to something I could only describe as what you might see in a horror movie. He didn't look like my husband at all. It was like looking at a stranger in my bed, which was very scary indeed.

Suddenly aware I wasn't alone, I glanced over my shoulder and saw my sister at the door with a look of horror etched on her face.

"It's okay," I said softly, beckoning her in.

She stood beside me, her hand placed protectively on my shoulder as we stared at this person who was Rick, but not him at all. We remained that way for what felt like ages, but which actually turned out to have been less than a couple of minutes. Then, his face changed again, resuming his peaceful expression. My Rick was back, but his breathing had changed. He was taking long, drawn out breaths.

The nurse who had remained there for the night called me out of the room. Sonia stayed, holding Rick's hand while I stepped outside.

"He won't live through the night," she said gently.

"I know," I said as the tears began to flow. "I know."

I slipped back into the room in time to hold Rick's hand as he took his last breath.

On May 30, 2016, at 1:50 a.m., my gorgeous, one-in-a-million husband passed away.

Chapter 5

WHAT DO I DO NOW?

It's hard to express the feeling of numbness in the days following Rick's death. You would think that after eleven months of living alongside someone with a terminal illness, somehow I would have been able to prepare myself for my husband's death. This couldn't have been further from the truth. It was almost like I was now living in an entirely different world. There was the before and the after. The after was a horrible, dark, desperate place that plunged me into depths of despair I had never imagined I could experience.

I have no idea what I expected I would feel like, but what I did know is that I didn't think the shock of it would hit me like it did. I mean, how could it? The sense of disbelief that Rick was no longer there or that he would never, ever walk through that door again was unbearable. The day following Rick's death I was consumed by such a feeling of sheer agony and longing to have him back; it was indescribable. A tsunami of emotions ran through me. All I could do was scream and cry like a wounded animal. I was consumed by anger at the world for taking such a wonderful husband and father away from us.

Visiting Rick's room induced an almost overwhelming swell of mixed emotions. On the one hand, it was comforting. I had always felt close to him there, and if I really strained, I could almost smell his familiar scent. On the other, I really struggled with the fact that although he had gone, all of his belongings were still there. *How could he not be here when his possessions were still scattered around?*

Rick's iPad was still there on the side table. A quick glance showed me that there were dozens and dozens of unopened emails. *What do I do with all of these? What can I say?* I had to leave his room, shutting the door with an ominous thud behind me.

I stood in the hallway, not knowing which way to turn. I just didn't know what to do with myself, where to go, or what to say. It was such a strange, uncomfortable feeling, particularly after weeks and weeks of having such a purpose in life: to look after Rick and make his dying days as comfortable as possible. It's only really at times like this that you start to wonder what life is all about. We're here one minute and gone the next.

I reflected that we had allowed our lives to become so full of material items. There is so much stuff we accumulate in life that has no real meaning. During our years in the Middle East, Rick had always enjoyed a good salary. We weren't silly with the money and always made sure we had a good pot of savings, but just as importantly, we made sure we enjoyed life. That, for us, was living a five-star lifestyle—flying business class, staying in luxury hotels, and eating in good restaurants. The kids didn't really want for anything either.

It hadn't always been like this. Both Rick and I had been brought up in the North of England. If we wanted something, we had to work for it—and work hard. My own working life began at the age of twelve. I started off by delivering newspapers and then moved on to helping my aunt delivering milk. I can't imagine many youngsters nowadays finding these jobs ideal. I would be up at two o'clock in the morning and hopefully be finished by seven or eight o'clock and then home for a bacon sandwich. By the age of fifteen, I was washing up in a pub in the evenings after school or over the weekend. When I finished school at the age of sixteen, I had a full-time, apprentice

Saoirse Brown

office job but would still work as a waitress in the evening while also studying shorthand at college. All of this hard work paid off, though, and by the age of seventeen, I had bought my first house. Rick's childhood had been a little more privileged, but still, I know he worked for what he got.

In recent years, we'd been surrounded by luxury, which was the product of our hard work. We'd always been very grateful for how we were able to live and the lifestyle we were able to afford. Yet, none of it is ever going with you, and none of it really matters. Not anymore. Not when something like this happens. To some degree, it's meaningless.

Grief can come in all sorts of guises. The loss of a treasured pet, a divorce, the kids going off to university, losing a business deal, the list goes on. Was there anything to rival the loss of a loving husband, though? I doubted it.

I reflected on other moments in my life when I have experienced grief, wondering if I had learned anything from it that could help me now. I remembered the feeling of devastation when our dog Clay had to be put to sleep many years before. He had developed a tumor in his leg, and we'd sent him for immediate surgery. Unfortunately, the tumor had returned, and after much discussion between ourselves and the vet, it was agreed a second surgery wasn't an option. So, our beautiful German shepherd boxer, who had been part of our family for nine years, was put to sleep. At the time, I experienced so many irrational thoughts. As the vet took Clay away, I was thinking: *Where is he going? Will they feed him? I hope they give him water.*

There is no logic to grief.

In the flood of irrational thoughts that hit me after losing Rick, I wondered why no one ever really discusses grief. *Why is society so afraid to talk about it?* Everybody is going to experience death and grief at some point in their lives, so perhaps it should be part of the school curriculum. It's an uncomfortable subject, so uncomfortable, in fact, that some people would rather cross the street than walk past someone who has experienced a loss because they don't know what to say. But if it's spoken about more, then surely this will make it easier to come to terms with. Maybe it would have helped if I had an inkling of what to expect.

But then again, maybe it wouldn't.

Finding the strength to organize the funeral was my next task, which I suppose, more than anything, pulled me back from the brink. I had to focus. Rick needed a big send-off. There were plenty of people who had been kept at arm's length throughout his illness, and they were determined to say goodbye properly.

Funnily enough, there was never any question as to which funeral parlor we would use. That had already been decided. For the past couple of years that we had lived in Surrey, Rick, had regularly pointed out a funeral parlor in a local village not far from our home. I always used to remark how strange it was that he would make such a thing about it and wondered why it seemed to draw his attention. Once, when we drove past and he didn't see it, he panicked and asked where it had gone. Of course, it hadn't gone anywhere. He had just missed it. Now, there was no question about it. I knew I needed to use this one.

Rick had also made another request about his funeral a couple of years earlier. Certainly, well before he knew he was ill. He had been asked to relocate for a short period to Houston, Texas, in the United States. His company wanted him to do some troubleshooting in their office there. Rick had always liked a challenge and fancied a few months living and working in the States, so he agreed. Of course, his beloved guitar went too, and he enjoyed playing his guitar just as much over there. When the weekend arrived, he had a well-worn routine of having a drink of his favorite whiskey, a twenty-one-year-old Glenfiddich, while playing his guitar. After he'd finished playing, he'd pour himself one more Glenfiddich, which he called his one for the road, even though he was already home, and would switch to listening to music for a short while. One of the bands he enjoyed was The Offspring, and in particular a song called "Gone Away." He played it regularly and then moved on to playing a version

SAOIRSE BROWN

of the same tune by the American Rock band Noctura. The lead singer, Mandy Suiter, had a beautiful voice, and it produced a much softer version of The Offspring's song. Rick asked more than once during our stay in the United States if the song could be played at his funeral. I would have normally brushed it off, but he asked me so many times that I actually saved the music to my iPad, as I knew I would never remember the band's name. I told him at the time that it was a strange request, but I promised that I would play it if the time came.

Looking back at these two incidents, I wonder if Rick had a premonition of his early death. Or maybe he had some sort of feeling deep in his subconscious and just wasn't aware of it.

Rick's funeral was held on June 10. I'd hoped I'd be able to hold it all together for the day, but when I glimpsed the hearse driving down our street, it was too much. I felt physically sick, light-headed, and very anxious. It took all my strength to climb into the car and compose myself for the drive to the crematorium. Once we reached the crematorium and were waiting for Rick's coffin to be brought out of the hearse, I lost it again. I became breathless, and my legs became weak. I knew I was really struggling now, and I leaned on my sister-in-law Gillian for support.

"I can't do it," I sobbed.

"You can," she replied, squeezing me close to her.

All I wanted was for someone to take the pain away. I didn't want to be there, but at the same time, I did. More than anything, I just didn't think I had the strength to continue with the day.

Running away was never an option, so I had to dig deep and find reserves of strength and courage that would see me through the next few hours. It was crucial that however much I suffered, I put my children first and stayed strong for them. What was happening now was happening whether I liked it or not. It was a surreal moment that needed to be lived, however awful.

Thoughts flooded into my head as we stood in the incongruously hopeful bright summer sunshine. *How can this be real? What am I doing here? Why is my husband laid in a coffin at such a young age?*

As the pallbearers lined up, I once again composed myself and steadied my breathing. The sight of our son, Jack, taking his place among the pallbearers made me flush with pride. *If he can get through this and do that, then I have to do this,* I told myself. I knew how difficult a thing it was for him to do, but he had insisted on it. Our daughter, Ellie, had been incredible too. She'd always had a very mature attitude and had been a rock in the past week.

I smiled as I remembered something Ellie had said on the day Rick died.

"Although he died far too young, aged just forty-seven years old, he lived the life of a ninety-year-old," she'd said with solemn assurance.

She was spot on too. Rick truly lived, grabbing every opportunity with both hands and living his dreams. We needed to celebrate that.

I was almost shocked as I walked into the crematorium. There were so many friends and family there who had come to say their goodbyes. Among them were friends he hadn't seen for years, and many who had traveled from overseas. It was almost overwhelming to see how Rick had affected so many people with his beautiful and generous nature, and it was just wonderful to see so many friends come together to pay their respects. It was going to be a difficult day for everyone who had known and loved him, not just his immediate family.

I don't remember a great deal about the service, which was a blur of emotion. Hearing "Gone Away" was just one of many moments that brought tears to my eyes. I had written a eulogy for Rick but found myself unable to deliver it, so my brother John kindly spoke on my behalf.

The tears didn't stop at the wake afterward, but I think we made a good fist of celebrating Rick's life, just as he would have wanted. There was a definite lighthearted undertone as we all shared our Rick

SAOIRSE BROWN

experiences. Everyone had a story to tell, which was entirely fitting. Rick had always been a big character and a very good storyteller, which is why he was always the center of attention. That day was no different.

I had arranged for a large picture of Rick to be placed on an easel at the entrance to the room where the wake was held at the Woodlands Park Hotel in Cobham, along with a memory book for all guests to sign. Oddly, and I'm not sure how, his picture fell off the easel a few times for no discernible reason. Several people saw this, and each one was adamant that no one had been close to the picture when it happened. There was no noticeable draft or gusts of wind either. Eventually, it became a bit of a running joke.

"Here's Rick again," we'd say. "Always wanting to be the center of attention."

As I shook my head in mock exasperation, I did wonder if maybe Rick hadn't gone so far after all. I told myself it was wishful thinking, but there was still a part of me that didn't think it was entirely impossible.

As any bereaved person will know, the days that follow a funeral can be almost as tough as the ones that immediately follow a loss. Once all the hard work of organizing a funeral, getting death certificates, and informing the relevant authorities is done, there is little left to do. Except think. And miss the person who has left a great big hole in your life.

It was just so quiet as Ellie, Jack, and I did our best to just comprehend the enormity of what had just occurred and get back into life without Rick being around anymore. As a family, we had always spent a lot of time apart. Rick had spent many years offshore, working on the oil rigs, so I was used to him working away. In his later years, he had spent more time in the office, so we were used to having him around a lot more. That said, the kids didn't see so much of him. They had gone off to boarding school for their senior years, as we never knew where we would be from year to year, so it made sense the kids were settled into one school to finish their education and take their exams. Even though we were used to being independent, and our circumstances frequently changing, this change was going to take a lot of getting used to. We were going to have to learn to live a new kind of life, which meant an overhaul, or a stripping back of what we knew. That was, of course, easier said than done.

We were fortunate enough to receive an immense amount of love and support from friends and family. There were many dinners cooked and dropped off for us and our shopping delivered. Cooking is the last thing you wish to be doing when you are grieving, so this thoughtfulness was received with such gratitude.

We didn't want to go anywhere. We'd much rather sit at home and just be with our emotions and one another. I would spend hours in Rick's room, looking around at all his things and wondering how I was ever going to come to terms with the loss of my husband. Someone I had spent so many years of my life with was just gone. I'd stare at his guitars hanging from the wall, trying to digest that these would never be played by him again. Knowing he wouldn't be coming back but his belongings would be staying was unbearable. Grief, that insignificant five-letter word that no one ever talks about, had hit me like a freight train, knocking me senseless and turning my life upside down. I knew that, somehow, through all that distortion, I had to learn how to stop it from taking hold of me and defining who I was. But how? I felt completely powerless.

I tried my best to keep to my normal routine, walking the dog and keeping up with my daily ritual of cleaning the floors, but some days were just too much. Nothing seemed normal anymore.

One day, after finding it particularly difficult to force myself out of the house, I mopped the floor vigorously on my return, perhaps in another futile bid to shake myself up and into action. I wasn't sure if that was true, though. In fact, I wasn't sure about anything anymore. Feeling slightly hot and even a little out of breath by my exertions, I stood back to survey my hard work.

How odd. There were footprints all along the floor where it was still wet. Not muddy footprints, but prints like someone had picked their way across the floor just after it had been cleaned, picking up a little water residue on the soles of their bare feet. I decided it must have been me, thanks to my energetic way of cleaning the floor that day. Even so, I was pretty sure I hadn't walked over my newly cleaned floor.

A few days later there was another strange occurrence. Jack kept his drum kit in Rick's guitar room, although he rarely played now. I was sitting alone in the next room when I heard the drums start up. It was a distinctive popular knock pattern: five knocks, pause, another two knocks. It's known as "Shave and a Haircut" or "Two Bits," and it's the knock you typically use when knocking on someone's front door. That was all fine. I've never minded a bit of music in the house. Except I was the only one there that morning. *What was going on?*

The drumbeat stopped as abruptly as it began, so I began to question if it had happened at all. I was convinced it had, though. I wasn't scared—just curious.

A few days later, Jack had decided to go out with some friends for a drink. He'd asked if I would pick him up later that evening from his friend's house, and I'd agreed. As it was nearing midnight, I decided to sit on the bed, relax, and read while I waited for his call. I'd barely stretched out before I heard the sound of a woman singing. She had a beautiful voice and was accompanied by a classical guitar. I knew it wasn't coming from my house: there was nobody else in that evening. I glanced over at my bedroom window, which was firmly closed. *Perhaps the neighbors had friends over and were making a night of it.*

I listened to the music, which was lovely. It had a calming, melodic quality that was almost soporific. I'm sure I would have fallen asleep listening to it if the phone hadn't rung with Jack requesting his pickup. I jumped up and out of bed, grabbed my car keys, and went outside. To my immense surprise, the road outside was completely silent. The neighboring houses were cloaked in darkness, their curtains firmly closed. Definitely no partying going on there, just sleeping. How very odd. *Where had that music come from?*

I collected Jack, drove home, and headed back to my bed. It had been another long day, and I knew I would be up early the next morning. I saw that Maisy was already curled up and settled for the night at the foot of the bed. That was good to see. She was usually a very insecure dog and always followed me around the house, getting desperate if I left her field of vision even for a moment, so it always gave me a warm feeling when I saw her so comfortable.

Jack popped into my room to say goodnight and stopped to stroke Maisy. He briefly spoke of his evening out and about some of the new people he had met. As he started to walk toward the bedroom door, I called out.

"Come and lie on the bed with me for five minutes. Let's have some delicious."

Jack rolled his eyes, and we both laughed. Rick and I used to have our own pet names for each other, as most couples do, and special little things we'd always say to one another. Whenever I wanted a cuddle, I would ask Rick for some delicious. Delicious was basically spooning. Jack must have been feeling the need for a hug too, as he willingly lay on the bed next to me, and we laughed again about how we could call a hug delicious.

Suddenly, I heard the same woman singing and the same guitar playing.

"Can you hear a woman singing?" I asked Jack.

Jack paused and listened.

"Nope," he said. "There isn't a woman singing. I can't hear anything."

He didn't ask me anything about what I could hear, and I didn't say anything. I'm not sure what I could have said anyhow. After Jack took himself off to bed, I was once again left wondering what was going on with these strange incidents.

Of course, I questioned whether anything was happening at all. Jack hadn't heard anything; maybe I was just imagining it. My husband had just passed away, and I wasn't exactly thinking straight. I had never been through grief like this before. *Maybe I just didn't want to let go? Maybe I would never really be ready to let go?*

That night I had the strangest dream about Rick, which as I later learned was to be the first of many odd dreams about my husband. In this dream, Rick arrived in my room and told me he was taking me to a party. Off we went, and Rick, being his usual jovial, sociable self, was so excited to be showing me all of the new people he had met. As we walked through the crowds of people, I asked him who they all were.

"He is a spirit, she is living, he is living, she is a spirit …" he said, pointing them out one by one.

Rick seemed so happy, and it all felt so real.

A couple of nights later, Rick turned up in my bedroom while I was sleeping. I'm not sure whether I was in a dream state or wide awake, but I felt myself wake up with a start to find him nudging me. He was trying to usher me over to his side of the bed.

"Move up, Mrs.," he laughed.

In another dream on another night, I heard a telephone ringing, and I picked it up in our bedroom. Rick was on the other end telling me he was okay and that he was in the garden. I asked him why he was phoning if he was in the garden and that I would be downstairs shortly. When I arrived downstairs, I looked into his office, and he was sitting on his chair like he always used to, smiling broadly. I knew then he was happy.

Ellie told me she had a couple of dreams too, where her dad had shown her how he had passed over. He showed her a brilliant, beautiful white light that she said was full of such love, she had never felt anything like it. She had always had such fear of death so felt this experience to be very comforting.

When I awoke each morning and replayed the dreams in my mind, I began to question what was real and what wasn't. Maybe I wasn't dreaming but was, in fact, meeting my husband on some sort of astral plane. Perhaps my thought of Rick being present at his own funeral wasn't so far-fetched after all.

This state of affairs continued. I began to get quite used to bumping into Rick all over the place. I looked forward to it even. I didn't tell anyone, though. I wasn't quite sure what sort of reaction I'd get.

After five weeks of losing Rick, Karen and David asked me to join them on a trip to Dubai. Karen and David were friends we had met while we were all living in Doha. We were all from the north and had always kept in touch even though we had left the Middle East to come back to the UK at different times, and we had ended up living around the corner from one another in Surrey. David had a meeting there, and Karen thought it would do me a world of good to take a break and hang out with them for a while. My head was filled with dozens of reasons why this was a terrible idea. I really didn't want to go. Apart from anything, it seemed just too soon to leave the kids. Yet, Rick's words kept coming back to me.

Spend a couple of months with Karen and David. You will be okay.

In the end, remembering my husband's words outweighed my doubts, and at the last minute, I decided that I would go with them. I also reasoned that the trip would allow me to see friends who had been unable to make it to Rick's funeral.

I was glad I agreed to go. Those few days away were a real tonic and gave me a nice opportunity to relax and unwind a little. I met up with our overseas friends and really enjoyed spending time sharing our memories of Rick. It was a lovely reminder of how greatly he had been loved by so many.

Before I left, I had imagined that the trip to Dubai would be very difficult because Rick and I had spent so many years of our married life in the UAE. Rick always saw the UAE as his first home even though I preferred the UK and missed the distinctive seasons. He loved everything about it over there. As it turned out, the trip was much easier than I had thought. I had mentally prepared myself for saying my goodbyes to that life, thanking it for all it had given us

SAOIRSE BROWN

over the years, including the friends we had met who were more like family. As most expats would undoubtedly agree, the bond you form with friends in a foreign land and build is special. The opportunities we had been given, the easy and carefree life, were remarkable. I was grateful for them all.

I did, however, find the final night difficult. I felt an overwhelming need to stay in my room alone with my thoughts of Rick. I needed the space to accept how I was feeling, realize my emotions alone, and then prepare myself to fly back to the UK.

The following day, when I arrived at Dubai airport, I felt much better. I was also very excited to be going home to see the kids. In fact, as I boarded the flight with Karen and David, I felt much more upbeat than I had in a while. We settled in our seats, and after a brief discussion about which movies we were going to watch with dinner, I settled down for the takeoff.

The movie I chose was okay, but certainly not as interesting that I would be prepared to watch another. Once the titles began to roll, I signaled to Karen that I was going to go to the bar at the rear of the plane to have a drink.

I was quite happy to go alone to the bar. Of all the years Rick and I spent in the Middle East, I had hosted dozens of parties and was always quite relaxed about socializing with people I didn't know all that well, even though I was never as outgoing as Rick. Luckily, I found none of my confidence had gone, and I went straight into chatting with the others at the plane's bar. I began talking to a couple on their way home after visiting their son in Australia and a female journalist who was terrified of anything that even hinted at turbulence. She seemed utterly convinced that the plane would go into a nosedive at any moment. There were another three other gentlemen whom I didn't really get to speak to until one of them introduced himself to me.

The man said his name was Simon, and for some reason, I seemed to form an instant opinion of him: small in height, not the best looking, but certainly not unattractive, and maybe a little overweight. I giggled to myself as the summary flitted through my brain. I had just described how I saw myself!

By the time Karen and David joined me at the bar, I was chatting and enjoying a drink with Simon. Simon told me he was divorced but would like to remarry one day, and I began to explain about Rick and his death a few weeks earlier.

"I don't think there will ever be a need for me to marry again," I said with total conviction. "As far as I'm concerned, marriage is about having children, and I have no desire for any more."

"Really?" frowned Simon. "I think there is more to marriage than that."

A lively discussion on the whys and wherefores of marriage ensued, which became so passionate that others in the bar weighed in with their opinions. Soon we were a lively group, chatting like we'd known each other forever, and another round of drinks was ordered.

It seemed like the most natural thing in the world for us all to clash glasses and say cheers. It's what you do in merry company, right? As we picked up our glasses and Simon walked closer, the tinkle of one glass meeting another began, with hearty cries of, "Cheers!" I then remembered something Karen always said.

"You've got to look people in the eyes when you say cheers," was her constant mantra. "Or it isn't really meant."

I was always sure to do it; otherwise, I'd risk the billionth repetition of the mantra in admonishment.

"Cheers!" I called out, laughing as my glass careered into Simon's out-held glass.

At the same time, I looked straight into his eyes.

Boom.

The laugh died on my lips. *What in the world?* I can hardly describe the feeling, but I instantly knew this man and trusted him 100 percent. *But how?* It was intuitive. I had been speaking to this man from across the bar for at least an hour and *did not* have any connection whatsoever. *What had just happened when I looked into his eyes?*

I tried desperately to pick up the thread of the marriage conversation as my head spun. Meanwhile, I did my best to avoid all further eye contact, which is never easy in a social situation and felt even more awkward after what had just happened.

"I think you should find a partnership that will last," I managed to stammer out. "You need some sort of yin and yang in a relationship."

I stole a glance at Simon's face and saw he was staring right at me.

"I am going to marry you," he said.

He looked utterly serious.

How ludicrous, I thought.

"I've told you. I'm not marrying again," I replied, laughing nervously.

"I am going to marry you," he repeated.

He was not laughing at all. Simon must have repeated the line about marrying me five times after that, and each time I told him it wasn't happening.

In the end, he said: "Let's agree to disagree."

For some crazy reason, we high-fived on it.

By now, I was feeling a little uncomfortable and awkward, so I very deliberately turned my back on Simon and engineered a conversation with my friend Karen. My husband had just passed away, and I didn't need any weird emotions coming into play right now.

Then, Simon just tapped me on the shoulder and said he wanted to get some sleep before the journey ended. Not long after, Karen and I finished our drinks and went back to our seats to relax a little before we landed.

As I settled back into my seat, I couldn't help but feel that I had been rude in the way I had ended the conversation with Simon. It wasn't in my nature to behave like that. I always did my best to be polite to everyone I met and certainly didn't relish making anyone feel bad.

After mulling it over for a while, I decided to find him and apologize. I had no idea where he was sitting but decided it wouldn't be that hard to look. After all, he wasn't going to leave the plane until it landed. I walked back through the plane, and when I eventually found where he was seated, I discovered he was asleep.

For reasons I can never explain, I knelt down beside Simon and stroked his arm a few times. He was obviously deeply asleep because he didn't respond at all. I reached out and took his hand in mine. Even as I looked down at our entwined fingers, I had no idea why I was doing what I was doing. Yet, it just felt so natural. *Why did holding his hand feel as familiar as holding that of my husband?* While he slept, he looked so beautiful. *Who was this man?*

I left without waking him up.

When I eventually arrived home, I was very confused about the encounter with Simon. Nonetheless, I sent him a message to say I had enjoyed talking to him and that further down the line it would be nice to meet up for a drink. Then I moved on with my day, preparing for some friends from Doha who were about visit.

Chapter 6

THE RIGHT PATH

Back in my usual haunt of Rick's room, surrounded by the ghosts of my past, I willed myself to pick myself up and find some purpose in life. It was what Rick would have wanted—I knew that. Sure, I'd had moments of happiness in the past few weeks. I had even found myself laughing a few times, which was something I thought would never, ever happen again. But all the time there was something there, pulling me back from the real world—a great big Rick-shaped hole.

We'd been through so much, Rick and me. It was impossible to imagine life without him. Every day with him had been such an adventure. I'd known from the first moment I had clapped eyes on him all those years before that he was the man for me.

I smiled as I remembered our first evening together. Anyone looking on would have been amazed that we'd found such a strong, enduring bond. Rick hadn't exactly looked like a prime catch at the time—far from it, in fact.

I was just twenty-two years old and on a night out with my good friend Julie. We worked at Roxburgh Electronics in Scunthorpe and had decided to hold our own impromptu office Christmas party. Our other colleague Fraser was supposed to be joining us but had changed plans at the last moment because his friend Rick was making a surprise visit. We talked about canceling the night out for about a nanosecond but decided very quickly that we were all revved up for a great evening so we'd go anyhow. It had been a while since I had been out dancing, and well, it was the festive season. I'd been working so hard all year too, juggling two jobs and my college work, so I'd really been looking forward to letting my hair down for an evening.

We met up at one of my favorite pubs, and pretty soon we were having a great time, knocking back drinks and chatting. About an hour after we arrived, the door opened, and in walked Fraser to a large cheer from our little crowd.

"You made it!" we shouted, almost in unison.

Fraser grinned broadly as he walked over, and we saw he had his mate in tow. It was also easy to see both of them were more than a little worse for wear.

"Couldn't let you all down," Fraser said, slurring his words slightly. "This is Rick."

Rick stepped out from behind Fraser and grinned lopsidedly.

"Hello," he slurred with a comical wave.

This one is more sloshed than Fraser, I thought. They'd obviously both been drinking for quite a while.

"Well, hello, Rick," I said with a smile.

Rick smiled back, and I couldn't help but notice he had the most beautiful brown eyes, like deep, dark pools with just a trace of a mischievous twinkle. He had beautiful, long, dark hair that perfectly framed his face.

He turned out to be a lot of fun too. After another round was bought, we resumed our banter, and despite being new to the group, Rick gave as good as he got. My sides ached I laughed so much. When Rick disappeared to the gents, Julie nudged me and smiled.

"You seem to be getting on pretty well there," she pouted.

"I like him." I shrugged. "He has lovely eyes."

When I had walked out of my front door that evening, I had no thoughts of getting into a relationship. Nothing could have been further from my mind. I was too busy keeping my head down and working hard. Now, though, I wasn't so sure.

The evening continued to go well, and I spent a lot of time talking to Rick even though he was definitely very drunk by now and getting more so by the minute. When Fraser declared we should get a pizza after the publican called last orders, I was the first to say yes.

"We can eat them at my place," Fraser said. "I think I've got some beers there too."

A short while later, after a lot of staggering around the high street, we arrived back at Fraser's small, semidetached house clutching a stack of brown cardboard pizza boxes. Each one of us collapsed on any available seating point and started to eat the lukewarm pizzas. Strangely, they weren't too bad either.

"Uh-oh," Fraser exclaimed. "That's not good."

We all turned to look in the direction of his gaze and burst out laughing. Rick was quietly vomiting into the box containing his half-eaten pizza.

"Ew," Julie and I chorused.

Maybe the pizzas were not so good after all.

"That's disgusting," Julie added.

By now, Rick was so drunk he seemed oblivious to the fact we were even in the room with him. He was staring into his pizza box in an almost catatonic state.

"Shouldn't someone take the box away from him?" I asked. "You know, before he drops it onto the floor."

Too late. Rick and the pizza box toppled onto the floor with a thud. Despite the fact that he was pretty far gone himself, Fraser leapt up and scooped the pizza box full of vomit up and firmly shut the lid.

"Yay, well done," we laughed.

It was all a bit disgusting, yes, but quite comical too.

I glanced down at Rick, who had curled into a ball on the floor. His eyes were tightly shut, and he appeared to be in a deep sleep.

"Seriously?" Julie giggled. "What is wrong with your mate, Fraser?"

I smiled as everyone teased Fraser and glanced down at the slumbering form. I fought a strong urge to go over, stroke his back, and make sure he was okay. I knew he hadn't exactly acquitted himself well that evening, and 99.9 percent of girls would not have seen him as boyfriend material, but I felt a strong connection to him. There was something special about Rick. I just knew it.

Rick must have felt it too because the following day he called. He said he wanted to apologize for his behavior, but we both knew it was just an excuse to speak to me again. He hadn't phoned to say he was sorry to Julie—let's put it that way.

"Can we meet up?" he said, once he had got through groveling for the pizza incident.

Of course, I said yes straight away. From that moment on we were inseparable. Rick was even more lovely sober than he was drunk.

We seemed to just fit together. We were both the same age and fiercely ambitious. What's more, we were both prepared to work hard for what we wanted, although Rick was far more confident and outgoing than I was. I also found it attractive that he was very evidently the sort of guy who said he was going to do something and then went on and did it. I had met plenty of people who talked the talk, but he seemed to be someone who was ready to go out and grab life to get what he wanted. He told me that he had moved to Abu Dhabi, UAE, with his parents when he was very young. His mother and father had emigrated there for work, taking Rick and his two sisters. He smiled as he said that he had always enjoyed the lifestyle out there, especially the warm weather.

"The next opportunity I get to go back out there to live and work, I'll be off like a shot," he said.

I didn't doubt it.

Rick explained that his career options had been a bit curtailed because he hadn't done brilliantly at school.

"My folks had this great idea of sending me here, to the UK, to finish school," he said shaking his head. "It was a disaster. I hated it. Half the stuff I had done wasn't on the curriculum, and I had never even seen some of the things they were banging on about it. Not surprisingly, I messed up my exams completely. My parents were pretty cross about it."

Showing real grit and determination, Rick threw himself into work on the rigs. It was all about his long-term plan to get back to the UAE, and he was prepared to start at the bottom of the career ladder to do it. I had to admire him. He'd recently been promoted to assistant driller, which he said was quite an achievement in such a short amount of time.

I couldn't get enough of my lovely, funny, charming Rick. Even though I'd met him just a few days earlier, I already felt like I had known him all my life. I was desperate to spend more time with him, even though it seemed impossible. He lived in a different county and was due to go back to Yorkshire imminently to spend time with his sister over Christmas. His nan, Jessie, who he and his sister currently lived with, had decided on some winter sun and had only recently flown over to Abu Dhabi to be with Marion, Rick's mother. Rick didn't want to leave his sister home alone for Christmas Day.

"Come with me to Yorkshire," he said suddenly, looking intently into my eyes.

There was no question whatsoever that I would say yes.

Naturally, everyone thought I was mad.

"Are you crazy?" my sister Sonia almost shouted. I was living with her and my brother-in-law at the time after selling my own house, and we had been planning our own family Christmas.

"You barely know the guy. He could be an axe murderer for all you know."

I did my best not to laugh. But I was so certain about Rick and the fact that he was the guy for me. He definitely wasn't a criminal either.

If Sonia and my other friends thought I was crazy disappearing off for Christmas with a man I had just met, they were even more exasperated by my next move. After a lovely time in Yorkshire with Rick, we decided to move in together. Permanently.

"It's only been a fortnight!" Sonia said. She was almost in tears. "Why does it have to be this quick? Spend some time getting to know each other first, and then, if it still feels right, you can think about living together."

But it did feel right then. It was perfect. I knew I wouldn't feel any differently in a month or a year's time. Why wait?

We decided to base ourselves in Scunthorpe because Rick would be working away on the rigs for a lot of the time and was regularly flying out of Humberside Airport, which was just up the road. It seemed to make sense that we were close to my workplace, and then he could come back whenever he could. We moved in with Fraser and a friend of his, but they moved out quite quickly because they wanted to be closer to their families back in Yorkshire. So, it was just the two of us, living in utter bliss.

We got into a routine, which was to become very familiar over the years. Rick would go offshore to the rigs for two weeks and then return home for two weeks. The two weeks he was away were always tough. I missed him so much. Communications were more complicated back then than they are now too, so I rarely got to speak to him in this period. The only option was to write a letter because calls to the only available landline were only supposed to be made in an emergency situation.

I used to count down the days until he returned to me. My employers at Roxburgh Electronics were really kind and would let me leave at lunchtime on the days Rick was due home, as long as I made up the time at a later date. I would climb into my car for the journey to the heliport to collect him, my stomach filled with butterflies of anticipation. We would always go straight from the heliport to lunch at a quiet pub somewhere to catch up. We would talk and talk, our hands entwined as we reveled in being together once again.

There was never any question that it might not work out in either of our eyes, and pretty soon, everyone around us accepted that too. Our friends and family could see how close and in love we were. No one batted an eyelid when we announced we were going to buy a house together. It just seemed to be the next logical step. By this stage, Rick had had yet another in his line of rapid promotions at work, and I had moved on from my job at Roxburgh Electronics and started a job with Europcar, a car rental company. I was a receptionist at Europcar's Humberside Airport desk, and then I was quickly promoted to manager. It was the ideal job for me because I loved working with the public.

The property we chose was close to the airport—convenient for my work and also for Rick's flights in and out every fortnight. Perfect. It was a large, three-bedroom, detached house with a little bit of land. The view from the rear windows was breathtaking because we looked over the rolling fields beyond. My favorite season was definitely spring when the farmer would move his lambs into the nearby field. I could have stood at the window for hours, watching them gamboling around, playing with one another, and then butting into their poor mothers for a top-up of milk.

I often used to pinch myself at the size and location of the house we were living in. I had never imagined owning something like it. Sure, a lot of our furniture was borrowed and secondhand because we'd spent every last penny on the deposit, but it felt like we'd really made it. We had huge plans for what we wanted to do with the house but were prepared to wait until we had enough time and money to do it properly. We couldn't resist doing a bit of DIY and decorating it by ourselves, though, as we saved up for the big projects.

It wasn't all hard work. We valued Rick's two weeks at home and were sure to spend as much time as we could together. Rick always had long lists of things he wanted to do too, although there never seemed to be enough time to fit it all in. I was really happy when he fulfilled one of his greatest ambitions, which was to start lessons to gain his pilot's license. Living so close to the airport meant we were in the perfect place for him to begin. I will never forget the day he took his first solo flight around the airport. I parked up outside the perimeter of the airport to watch, squinting up at the sky and trying to spot his plane. My heart soared as I did. I was so proud of him. Rick had so much drive. He always knew what he wanted and went for it.

Rick never lost sight of his dream to return to Abu Dhabi one day and still spoke of it often. There was never any question that I would go too, and whenever he talked about it, I wondered what it would be like. I wasn't sure how I would fare in the heat. I rather liked the British climate. However, if it meant being with Rick, I would have lived on Mars.

Quite a few of Rick's work friends were keen on a spell working in the Middle East too. It was quite a common career path for oil workers because it meant a few years working in a great climate for a tax-free sum. When a bunch of jobs came up in Abu Dhabi, a group decided to travel out there to check out the lay of the land and asked Rick if he'd like to go along. I wasn't aware of the conversation until a few days later, as it happened while Rick was on his two-week rotation offshore. However, he told me all about it when he made a sneaky call home from the rig. He wasn't supposed to make calls, but he said sometimes he missed me so much he just needed to hear my voice.

"I think I might go out there with them," Rick said. "Be interesting to see what jobs there are. It won't tie us into anything."

"Yes, it is a good idea," I encouraged him.

I paused, unsure of whether to say what was on my mind. I wasn't sure if it was a lads-only trip.

"Listen, I am happy if you say no, but I could come too," I said hesitantly. "I'm due some time off work, and I've always fancied going out there. It seems like a good opportunity."

"Perfect," Rick said. He sounded genuinely pleased too. "I'll get them to book you a ticket."

I was so excited about the trip. It had all happened so quickly. I couldn't believe that morning I'd just been going about my ordinary routine, and now I was due to be flying off to the Middle East in a couple of weeks. I'd finally get to see this place that Rick had been banging on about for a couple of years, and I would most likely meet his mother there too.

I phoned work and arranged for the time off and started to work out what to pack. I was just thinking that I might need to invest in a few floaty summer dresses when the phone rang again. It was Rick.

"Bit of a problem," he announced. "My friend went ahead and booked the ticket, but because he didn't know your surname, he put it in mine. Is there anything we can do about that?"

I giggled.

"Not to worry," I said. "What travel agent did he book it through? I'll give them a call and get the ticket changed."

I heard Rick fumbling around for the piece of paper that had all the details on it, and then he read the name of the agent to me.

"No problem. I'll give you a shout if there is an issue. I'm sure it will be fine."

As soon as we finished the call, I dialed the travel agent. The lady I spoke to couldn't have been nicer, except she delivered the news that the ticket alteration would cost fifty pounds.

"Fifty pounds?" I said. "That's ridiculous. It can't cost that much to reprint a ticket."

The lady started a well-worn lecture about admin costs and the like. I didn't pursue it. Having worked on the car hire desk for so long, I did empathize with her. It wasn't always easy to help customers at the same time as adhering to strict head office procedures.

I stood in the hallway, the phone receiver still in my hand, thinking hard. Out of nowhere, an idea popped into my head. *How much does it cost to get married at a registry office?*

I giggled as I looked up the number. *In for a penny, in for a pound. Why shouldn't I become Mrs. Howorth? We are all but a married couple anyhow.*

I dialed the number and got straight through.

"Can I ask how much it is to get married at a registry office please?" I asked.

"Certainly, it is sixty-five pounds," was the response.

I paused. But only for a second. It seemed like a no-brainer to me.

"Can I book a date please?" I said.

Moments later, I called Rick on the rig. These phone calls back and forth weren't the norm, but in my mind, this was as close to an emergency as it got.

After a few minutes, Rick came to the phone. I began a rapid explanation of the travel agent's admin fee and then dived right in with it.

"I also spoke with the registry office, and the fee to get married is only sixty-five pounds," I said breathlessly.

"So, Rick, we are getting married next week when you come home—a few days before we leave for Abu Dhabi," I added.

Complete silence. A million thoughts raced through my mind. Had we been cut off? That sometimes happened. Or was he furious at me for even suggesting this? Maybe this was never his plan, and he couldn't imagine marrying me at all. Or, perhaps he thought I was joking.

"I'm not sure about that," Rick began slowly, as though he were trying to take it all in.

I suppose I had rather sprang it on him.

"Well, if you are not sure by now, after two and a half years, then you are never going to be sure," I said, trying to sound far more confident than I actually felt.

Again, silence.

"Okay then," he said at last.

We were getting married.

SAOIRSE BROWN

Rick and I were married at the registry office on January 22, 1994. It was a very simple day with only a couple of family members present to witness the paperwork. We didn't even have time to arrange a proper wedding breakfast. Nor did we have wedding rings. We agreed that we would buy them while we were in the Middle East because the gold was a better karat out there and far, far cheaper. In the end, I used my sister's wedding ring for the actual ceremony. So many people had told us that it was bad luck, but that hadn't been the case in our marriage—far from it. We were, for the most part, very happy together.

A few of our friends and acquaintances were similarly negative about our hurriedly planned registry office wedding. Some even commented that we would regret having such a low-key ceremony one day.

"You'll look back and wish you had a big white wedding with all the works," I was told more than once.

I didn't dare say it, but I couldn't have imagined anything worse. Firstly, there's the huge waste of money for this one day extravaganza, and secondly, I have never liked being the center of attention. Just the thought of all those eyes turned on me turned my stomach. I was very happy that Rick and I had done it our way, making our vows and focusing on each other, just as it should be. I never had any regrets about it then or afterward.

A few days after the wedding we flew to Abu Dhabi. Rick's mother, Marion, collected us from the airport. To say she was shocked when Rick introduced me as her daughter-in-law would be an understatement. He'd kept the big news to himself until we'd arrived. Once she got over the surprise, she was very welcoming, and we had a great time in Abu Dhabi. I now completely understood why Rick loved the place so much.

The trip didn't turn into a job opportunity as hoped, although we both agreed it was an option that we'd very much keep open. We were happy enough to stay in the UK for a while and would take any opportunities as and when they came up.

One year later, we found out that we were expecting our first baby. It wasn't planned, but we hadn't taken any precautions to prevent it happening either, so it wasn't a complete surprise to us. Scary, yes; like most first-time parents we felt nervous, but it also seemed like a natural progression for us.

The pregnancy went smoothly. I was so relaxed and happy throughout it all, and Rick seemed pretty excited about being a dad. Deep down, I was secretly hoping for a boy and had even picked out the name Jack. Most of all, though, I just wanted a healthy, happy baby.

I loved my job so saw no need to finish work too early, especially since I felt well enough to continue. I carried on working full time right up until two weeks before the birth. On November 2, 1995, our little princess Ellie was born. As soon as I laid eyes on her perfect little face, the thought that I had been fixated on about having a boy evaporated from my head. She was beautiful—totally perfect in every way. She had a lovely, gentle temperament too and was such a good baby that we decided to try for another almost immediately. Thus, on February 27, 1997, our little soldier Jack was born. He had a thick shock of black hair and was as absolutely gorgeous as his sister.

Six months later, Rick received a call from a company in Abu Dhabi asking him if he would like an interview for a job there. The firm explained that the position would accommodate the whole family going out there, which was a bonus, because often the jobs on offer were only for single males. We talked it through, decided that now was as good a time as any, and even if Rick didn't get this particular job, we'd move over there anyhow and start a new life.

My family was happy for us but a little upset too, not least because they would have liked time with the two little ones. I promised that, whatever happened, we'd be back in the UK by the time they were both old enough to go to primary school.

Rick got the job, and it was perfect. With Ellie now aged two and Jack aged six months, we packed our bags, rented our home in Scunthorpe, and moved out to the UAE.

SAOIRSE BROWN

As Rick had always promised, I fell in love with the Middle East. Life there was very different from living in the UK. We were treated like royalty everywhere we went. Everyone seemed so eager to help us and do things for us. Although initially I felt a little uncomfortable with this way of living, it was surprising how quickly I got used to it, and it became the norm. After a while, all thoughts of returning to the UK for anything other than a visit vanished from my head. Jack and Ellie never did enroll in their English primary schools. One year rolled into another, and we moved around the Gulf states with Rick's work. We loved our life and were blissfully happy.

It wasn't until eighteen years later that we finally returned to the UK for good. But that homecoming had been as far from perfect as it was possible to be. It was the time when I lost my cheeky, confident, oh-so-lovey Rick.

Chapter 7

■ ■■■ ■■■ ■■■ ■■■ ■■■ ■■■ ■■■ ■■■ ■■■ ■■■ ■

MOVING FORWARD

New Year's is often a time of deep reflection: when we look back at the events of the previous year and one's role in them and then look forward to the year ahead, working out what might be achieved. This went doubly for me on the first New Year's after losing Rick.

I wasn't short of invitations to go out and celebrate—far from it, in fact. My friends and family continued to be amazing. People say in jest that you can't choose your family, but if I had that choice, I would definitely choose the beautiful souls I have for my brothers and sisters and, of course, my children. I don't know where I would have been without them all; they truly were my rock.

However, I was adamant I wanted a quiet New Year's this time. Funnily enough, in recent years, Rick and I had chosen not to go out to celebrate New Year's, even though we always had plenty of parties to choose from. We found we preferred an early evening meal out followed by a couple of drinks at home. Now I had even less desire than ever to go out and celebrate the passing of another year, preferring instead to spend the evening in Rick's room, listening to music, and thinking of the wonderful years we spent together. I was so blessed to have this man in my life for so many years, and I wanted to be on my own to reflect on that.

Looking back on the past seven months, I wondered how much I had managed to move on. After the initial shock and grief had subsided a little, I had been determined not to let Rick's death define me. I felt certain he would have said that to me many times if he saw me withdrawing into my shell. In fact, I was convinced he did do just that, and many months earlier I had proof too.

I'd been sitting in his room, as I did on a daily basis, staring at his picture. I'd gotten into the habit of chatting to the picture and updating him on what was going on. The summer sun was still streaming through the window, radiating hope, yet I felt anything but confident for the future.

"So, what am I going to do now?" I asked the picture. "We spent twenty-four years together and had a wonderful life. I never once regretted giving up my job and moving to the Middle East, but where does that leave me now? What am I qualified to do?"

The words had barely come out of my mouth when I was distracted by a movement outside the window. I turned my head and saw a beautiful butterfly just outside the glass. As I did so, a thought popped into my head. I say *popped*, but it actually hit me with the force of a tsunami.

Without change, that beautiful butterfly wouldn't be there. It is time for you to make that change.

It was Rick talking to me. I just knew it.

Rick didn't want me to sit at home, mourning. He wanted me to invent a new life for myself and the children.

Even as I began to think about it, I suddenly felt more optimistic. It's strange, but the sensation of being more positive seemed to fuel itself after a while. Having stepped away from the downward spiral I had been in, I felt almost like I too had grown beautiful wings. I used to have a WhatsApp group that I had started a couple of years earlier, but gave it up when Rick had become ill. This was a place where people would post something they were grateful for each day. When I did it, it really did have a positive effect. The more I thought

SAOIRSE BROWN

about all the good things that happened, the more good things that seemed to happen. This was the same sort of thing.

Ideas about what I could do next began to flood my brain. I'd always been interested in psychology, so I decided to take a counseling course. It was a little daunting even thinking about going back to school, particularly since I hadn't worked for eighteen years. However, I knew intuitively this was something I needed to do and that it would help me move forward.

I also wanted to do some volunteering. I had always liked the idea of volunteering for Age Concern, but because we only intended on coming back to the UK on a sporadic basis, there was no way I could offer 100 percent commitment. Now, though, I thought back to the ninety-three-year-old I had met in the hospital waiting room while waiting for Rick's treatment. I'd been very sad to see that she had no one to accompany her to her hospital visits. She'd brushed aside my inquiries as to whether she would consider a befriender from Age Concern, but I was convinced she'd appreciate it if someone was there to lend some support.

I got in touch with Age Concern and offered my services. Almost immediately, I was put in touch with a ninety-year-old lady named Hazel who had lost her husband three years earlier. I made an appointment with her and went along to introduce myself, but from the beginning, Hazel was adamant that she really didn't need any help, just like the lady in the hospital.

"It's very kind, but I am absolutely fine," she insisted. "I am sure there are other people you should be visiting."

I didn't push too hard. I simply stayed, chatting about this and that. I talked a bit about the time I'd spent in the Middle East, which I think she found quite interesting.

"Listen, I have really enjoyed chatting with you today," I said after a while. "Could I just pop around next week? There's no harm in that."

And she relented.

I started visiting Hazel every week after that. She was a lovely lady and incredibly interesting too. She also soon began to enjoy my visits, and on some days, I would find her standing at the window looking up and down the street as she waited for my arrival.

With my days beginning to fill up, there was another ambition I decided to tick off: learning Spanish. I had always been envious of people who spoke languages fluently and had long wanted to be one of them. Now was the time to stop dreaming about it and get on with it. I signed up for a beginner's Spanish course and started it in September.

The strange encounters in the house, which had started innocently enough with the footprints, drum playing, the lady singing, and those dreams, had accelerated markedly. The next strange manifestation concerned the electrics in the house, which kept tripping, leaving the house in darkness and all our appliances juddering to a silent halt. We'd never had an issue with the electrics before and didn't expect to because we were living in a newly built house that was only four years old.

I was away visiting family up north and the children were working, so they stayed at home. The electrics had started tripping on a regular basis while I wasn't there, so I asked them to mention the problem to our neighbor, who also happened to be an electrician. He said he'd take a look.

"There's absolutely nothing wrong," he told them with a shrug. "I did all the usual tests and a few more besides and couldn't find a single issue. The wiring is completely sound and as it should be."

How odd. I returned home from my break up north, feeling a little confused about the electrics scenario while I had been away, but I went upstairs to unpack from my trip. I'd barely opened my case before the electricity tripped again. *Seriously?* I went back downstairs to flick over the trip switch and listened as everything rumbled back into life.

The electricity seemed to behave itself for the next day. Then, the following night I awoke with a start at two o'clock in the morning.

For a few moments, I couldn't work out what had woken me, and then I knew. The electricity was off again. The house had been plunged into complete silence. The usual hum of the fridge and freezer had disappeared, and the whole house was cloaked in a remarkable and strange stillness. No wonder I had woken up.

I picked up my phone, which was lying on the table by my bed, and flicked on the flashlight inside it. Swinging my legs around to the floor, I got up and headed for the door, using the light to guide me and stop me from bashing into things. After that, I picked my way gingerly down the stairs and headed down the hallway to the fuse box. It was such a familiar path, I was pretty sure I could have navigated it even without a flashlight, but I didn't wish for any accidents. Standing on tiptoe, I pulled open the fuse box door and peered inside.

Nothing.

Everything was as it should be—no tripped fuses. Frowning, I peered out of the window into the darkness. It had to be a general power cut, I figured. It was impossible to tell, though. Everyone's lights were off anyhow because it was the dead of night.

I closed the fuse cabinet door and headed back upstairs to my bed, wondering if I would be able to get back to sleep now that I was so wide awake. I'd barely climbed into bed and scooched down under the covers when I heard everything rumble back into life. The last thought that entered into my head before I fell asleep was: *That's great. I won't need to worry about the freezer food.*

The following morning, for no particular reason, I checked the fuse box again. I could hardly believe my eyes when I saw that one of the switches had tripped; yet, everything in the house was working perfectly. *What is going on?* There could only be one explanation: Rick was keeping in touch.

Or, perhaps it wasn't just Rick. I was increasingly coming to the conclusion that he was not the only person from the spirit world who was trying to communicate with me. One day, after I had spent a lovely time out in London with my sister Sonia, the strangest thing happened. We'd returned to my house and enjoyed a cup of tea and a chat before we both took ourselves off to bed. I could only have been under the covers for a matter of moments before, out of nowhere, I sensed a woman running up to my side. I barely had any chance to register shock or alarm before the woman let off an ear-piercing cackle right next to my ear. My first reaction was to laugh nervously, but then I realized I was terrified, so I leapt up and ran into Sonia's room and dived under her covers.

"What is it?" my sister said, peering down at me. "What's happened?"

"A woman … a spirit … She cackled," I managed to pant out breathlessly. "I'm not sleeping in there tonight."

Once I calmed down, I grew more accepting of my spiritual companion, but nevertheless felt it was a little unnerving for anyone to just turn up uninvited and cackle loudly in my ear. I think what disturbed me the most about the encounter was that all the other spiritual interventions had felt loving and gentle, whereas whoever was behind this one seemed a little malevolent.

As the year rolled on, first into autumn and then into winter, I had braced myself for the inevitable wobble that would occur as Christmas loomed. The first Christmas without a loved one is always tough. Not only that, but it was going to take a bit of getting used to being in chilly old England after years of enjoying the festive season in full sun. Still, Christmas had always been my favorite time of year, and I was determined to enjoy it. I'd always liked the thought of visiting a European Christmas market, so I persuaded my friend Karen to come with me to Brussels. Not that she needed much persuasion, we always enjoyed spending time together. It was a nice break and got me into the Christmas spirit as I hoped.

On Christmas day itself, some of my family and their partners came along and my lovely Age Concern lady Hazel did too. I had kept myself so busy with food preparations and making sure everyone was happy that I didn't focus too much on Rick not being present. It was only later in the day that I realized I had no need to

SAOIRSE BROWN

worry after all because the day went surprisingly well. Not for the first time, I reflected that I was blessed to be surrounded by such wonderful friends and family.

I felt the agonizing pressure of my grief slowly lift. I missed Rick every second of every day, but I also now believed I could get through it and somehow find the life I had lost. I never, ever lost the sense that, somehow, I was being guided on the right path. I felt comforted by the fact that Rick was not just a wonderful memory.

By now I was certain he was with me every single day.

As I reflected on my year, sitting alone in Rick's room on New Year's Eve, my thoughts slowly turned to one other person in my life—if *in my life* was the right expression. Simon, the guy I had met on the plane, had stayed in touch. We spoke now and again, just as friends. Nothing more than that was ever thought of, especially since I had lost my husband not long ago. At the same time, I was profoundly curious about that extraordinary connection we'd felt when our eyes met on the flight.

When Simon told me that he was presenting a business development course I hemmed and hawed as to whether I should go. I knew what he was teaching could possibly help with my own business development. So, after a bit more pontification, I decided I would go and asked Sonia to come with me.

I'd felt a little awkward when I arrived, and Sonia and I took our seats toward the back of the room. *Maybe this was a big mistake?* Even though I was nervous, I smiled as I turned to see Simon behind me, at which point he came over to say hi. We spoke for a brief while before he bounded onto the stage energetically and introduced himself to everyone there. It was good to see him again and hear his voice.

"And I would like to say a very special welcome to this lady, sitting there at the back," he said, pointing right at me.

I swear I blushed as everyone swiveled around in their seats to look at me.

That wasn't all. Without warning, he launched into the story of how we met on a flight from Dubai. He was seemingly oblivious to my squirming.

Simon had a lovely way of speaking, and soon everyone in the room was entranced by his welcome speech.

He moved seamlessly onto the subject of the talk. I relaxed a little in my seat as I listened to what he had to say. He certainly seemed very knowledgeable.

Suddenly, almost out of nowhere, he called out my name and asked me to stand up. This was a cue for everyone to swivel around in their seats again. In my embarrassment, I had completely lost the thread of what he was saying, but it had been something to do with being organized or keeping track or something like that.

He looked around at his audience, who seemed to be drinking in this rather odd scenario "So when I met her, I took the liberty of recording our conversation on my Dictaphone," he continued. "I wanted to be able to remember everything I said to this lady." He smiled, so I took that as a sign that he was joking.

Simon paused and looked straight at me.

"And I do remember every word," he said meaningfully.

Instinctively, I knew he was referring to the marriage part of our in-flight discussion.

"I also remember what my response was," I said, surprising myself at how clear and loud my voice sounded in this most cripplingly embarrassing situation in front of a room of strangers.

The members of the audience looked absolutely baffled by now and kept turning to look alternately between me and Simon. The guy who was sat on the other side of Sonia nudged her and said in a not-so-subtle whisper, "What's going on between them two?"

"Nothing," she replied. "They met recently."

Even so, she did shoot me a very bewildered look.

Simon continued to include me throughout the presentation, and I had little choice but to respond. The banter between us continued back and forth during the whole event.

There was no time to chat one-to-one afterward, as he had a line of people waiting to ask him questions. I left the event feeling more confused than ever. Nothing much seemed to make sense these days, that was for sure. While I had done so well at picking myself up and dealing with whatever life threw at me, I still didn't know for certain what the future held.

As I looked forward to my first full year alone, I couldn't help but feel a little apprehensive about what it all meant and what would happen next.

A lady I had met just recently suggested I may like to consider Reiki, which is a natural technique, delivering healing energy through the hands to another person. Reiki (meaning universal energy) was discovered by Japanese scholar Mikao Usui. A couple of people I knew who had already tried it had said it had managed to help them feel a lot calmer, easing any stress. I was also told it may help release some emotions while I was going through the grieving process. Anything I could find that would help me relax a little more could only be a benefit.

A brief search online found a Reiki practitioner named Pam who lived just a few miles away. To be honest, I had no idea what to expect as I tentatively approached the first session. She was very good, though, and put me completely at ease. Almost immediately, I felt a wonderful warmth from her hands, which was like a glowing radiance flooding through my body.

"I feel a lot of emotions," she said in a calm, melodic voice. "Mostly down the side of your body."

I wasn't particularly surprised to hear this. After the year I'd had it seemed inevitable that I would be filled with a heady cocktail of powerful emotions. It was lovely to feel such a connection with someone, though, and without a doubt, she created a real feeling of peace, security, and well-being. As we chatted afterward, I had an overwhelming sense that I had been guided to find Pam. It was yet another spiritual intervention in my long recovery. I also believed that I had found another friend in Pam.

By this stage, I was intensely curious about all the spiritual activity around my life. I felt no reason to fear it. Other than the cackling woman, it all seemed benign. However, I couldn't shake the feeling that someone was trying to tell me something, but I just didn't have the right tools to understand what it was he or she was trying to say. I was very fortunate to be aware of the spirits that surrounded me, as not many other people are, but if the communication was only ever one way, it would be a real waste.

Once again, my spirits guided me to the right answer. When I say guided, I mean a thought just comes into your head, but you just know it's not your own thinking. It is difficult to explain to anyone who hasn't experienced it. The answer I was guided to this time was automatic writing. Until the idea was presented to me, I had never even heard of automatic writing. Once I did, I did some research and discovered it is a psychic ability that allows a person to produce written words without actually consciously writing. The words that come out of the exercise are produced by spirits.

Perfect, I thought. *Just what I have been looking for.*

Feeling a little nervous, I hunted in the drawer for a notepad and pen and settled down at Rick's office desk. *What now?* A thought popped into my head.

Ask a question.

My heart began to beat a little faster as I thought about what to ask. Okay, now I knew. I swallowed hard and opened my mouth to speak.

"Rick, are you still with us?" I said out loud, also writing it down, feeling a little unsettled as my words reverberated around the office.

The pen was in my hand, and I pressed the nib to the paper. To my astonishment, I began to write. Again, it is almost impossible to describe if you have never experienced this, but the words I started to write down were not being driven by ideas coming from my brain. They almost seemed to come from the pen itself.

"'Yes," spelled out the pen.

For a few moments, I stared at the notepad in shock and surprise. My mouth was dry, and I felt almost dizzy. *How was this even possible?* My brain was utterly unable to compute the enormity of what had just happened. Feeling overwhelmed, I threw the pen down and ran out of the room.

It took a little while to calm down, but once I did, I knew I wanted to try it again. I felt drawn to it. I needed to communicate with whoever wanted to speak with me. I had to do it.

Over the next few weeks, I tried automatic writing more and more. Initially, the conversation was with Rick. He was concerned about Ellie's relationship with her boyfriend. She had always been a daddy's girl, so this concern wasn't a shock to me. I continued to allow these gentle messages to come through, not just for Ellie but there were also some messages for myself and Sonia.

Suddenly, though, something changed. The tone and content of the messages altered abruptly. It was as though other spirits were trying to push through to say something. Rick seemed to disappear and female spirits arrived. They would take turns writing through me. There was one called Lou Lou who would explain about a spiritual awakening. She seemed intent on explaining that I was going home, drawing steps and infinity signs, and just giving general guidance on what was happening. She never bothered me. I had no idea what any of this meant. I just knew I had to research it. Then two others appeared, and they both obviously just wanted to have some fun. I believe one of the ladies was the one who cackled in my ear while I was in bed one evening. After allowing them to stay in my space for a few days, I decided I didn't want them around anymore. I was beginning to feel uncomfortable.

I knew then I had to give up automatic writing. The experience had been a huge learning curve for me. My desire to communicate with the spiritual world had started with the best of intentions, but I could see I had been a little naive. I hadn't really known what I was doing, and in my haste to speak with spirits, I hadn't really considered who I was connecting with or that not everyone would be full of love and kindness. It was a big lesson learned: when you decide to connect with the spiritual world, you must protect yourself and be aware of who you might be communicating with.

I consulted with a psychic lady I had met who explained what to do to get rid of the two mischievous spirits. I did as she instructed, and they departed. I had been keeping all the writing that I had done in journals, but I destroyed them all because I did not want anything more to do with it right then.

I'm not sure if it was this or the Reiki treatment I had received that had unlocked something, but by this stage, the house had become alive with spiritual activity. Some days it was just crazy. Lights would go on by themselves, an iPod player would start up and then abruptly stop, and snatches of laughter would drift through the air even though there was no one there. I would hear spirits talk to one another as if I weren't there. My bedroom was the worst place for such activity. I was frequently woken up in the night by spirits saying my name. Daily, when I lay in bed, I could see energy in my peripheral vision. One day, while changing my bedding, I sensed something to my left by the bedroom doorway. I glanced over and saw with my naked eyes a huge ball of energy swirling around.

"Well help me strip the bed then!" I joked, but it was a little unnerving.

These bizarre happenings were becoming my normal, though. The strange events weren't just confined to the house either. Whenever I drove my car, the windshield wipers would turn themselves on at random moments, and the fans and car radio would regularly go on and off for no discernible reason. I started to keep a journal of when and where everything happened.

Strangely, the only other person to witness anything was Ellie. Jack was always insistent there was nothing whatsoever wrong and said we were both imagining things.

Without a doubt, one of the most memorable moments was witnessed by both Ellie and me. We had been eating dinner in the kitchen, and I had left the table briefly to put something in the

SAOIRSE BROWN

sink. I was just turning back to walk over to the table when I saw something out of the corner of my eye. The can of Coke Ellie had been drinking moved—by itself.

"Mum, did you see that?" she asked slowly. "This empty Coke can has just moved on its own."

I stared at the can and nodded. "I saw it move, yes," I confirmed. "I thought you had pushed it up the table."

Ellie shook her head. She too was staring at the can. "I never touched it," she said quietly.

A thousand thoughts rushed through my head with a thousand reasonable explanations. Most likely of all was that it was a glass table and the Coke can had simply slid on some liquid below. Some of the drink had spilled, or perhaps there had been some condensation. Maybe Ellie had knocked it with her elbow but not really noticed. I knew for sure, though, that the table was level, so I needn't question that.

I had to find out what it was, though.

I walked over to the table and lifted the can. It was bone dry beneath. I knew we were both thinking the same thing because without saying anything, we both cleared everything from the table. Just to make sure, I wiped the can carefully, and Ellie dried it off with a cloth. I then carefully placed the can back on the table.

We both took a step back.

"Okay, if there is anyone in this room with us, please move the Coke can," I said loudly and clearly.

We held our breath.

Holy shit! The Coke can moved up to the other side of the table.

Talk about being excited. I leapt into the air, punching my fist, while Ellie told me to calm down.

"Calm down?" I practically shouted. "How can you be calm? Did you just see that?' I added, somewhat superfluously.

"I know. Oh my God," Ellie squealed. "Can you believe it?"

"Let's try again," I said. I had to be sure. "If there is anyone in this room with us, please move the Coke can," I repeated.

And it moved again. I asked the same question over and over again, and each time the can obediently shifted, just as before. What an experience! Like so many people, I had often asked the question: is there life after death, and if there is, why don't the dead show themselves? Now I had the answer. The definitive proof, not just for me but for Ellie too. If I never experienced anything paranormal again after that point, it would have been enough for me. I had seen all that I had needed to see.

As I looked back on all that happened to me in the months that followed Rick's death, through my gradual spiritual awakening, I realized the Coke incident together with the downward spiral of my experiments with automatic writing were a bit of a turning point. Although the developments both opened my eyes and answered many questions, they also marked a time that my curiosity became a little more realistic. I was not prepared to pursue the search for answers at all costs. The automatic writing had alerted me to the dangers of being too unguarded in my activities. Now I had been shown that there was hope, and I needed to think carefully about what I did next.

Being more cautious didn't mean I was no longer interested. I certainly wanted to know what the spirits wanted with me. I was aware this activity was fairly unusual and, I suppose, a little flattered that so many spirits seemed keen to communicate with me. However, I just wanted to take things one step at a time.

My most recent act had been to visit a spiritualist church to see if I could find any answers there. After all, if there was anyone who knew about what I had been through, it was highly likely they'd be found at a spiritualist church. I couldn't be the only person going through these experiences.

Sure enough, I was entirely right. On my first visit around a month earlier, I was happy to see that there were many more people like me who talked freely of their connection with the spirit world. I thought what I had going on around me was difficult to deal with, but there was one poor man who heard spirits talking all day long.

Saoirse Brown

He was there trying to find help on how to manage it. My heart went out to him. It couldn't be easy living like that.

The culmination of the meeting was when a person was invited onto the platform at the front of the church to receive and relay messages from the spirit world. There were no messages for me that time, but I was interested enough to go back a couple more times to listen to what others had to say.

I found it all quite comforting and would probably have continued to go there for much longer because it fit into my wish to take things slowly, keeping everything at arm's length for a while. However, that all changed when I was invited to be the one to go to the platform and receive messages.

At first, I was quite happy to do it. In fact, I found it remarkably easy to bring a message through. There were four mediums on stage, including myself. A spirit had come through for a lady in the audience. It had been brought through by one of the other mediums. We asked the spirit a couple of questions.

"Can you give your loved one a date?" was one of them.

It can be an anniversary, birthday, or anything significant really. Most of the time these dates resonate with whoever they are trying to communicate with.

"Do you have a gift to give to your loved one?" was another question we posed to the spirit.

My answer for the lady in the audience was that the gift was clear crystals, at which point she laughed and said she uses crystals for her angel card readings. She seemed quite happy with the response.

After we had finished with our messages, I sat down in one of the pews and watched other mediums for a little while. While sitting there, I randomly received a message for a woman sitting in front of me. Her granddad was wanting me to give her a gift of Marmite. I tapped her on the shoulder and asked her if it meant anything to her, she replied that she loved Marmite.

I quite enjoyed being the person who was able to give the much-waited-for message to a loved one, however odd the message might be. Then, later in the evening, a few of us went into another room, and one of the organizers asked me to bring someone through. I did, and it turned out to be a young girl. She was wearing a white dress and was probably just twenty or twenty-two years old at most. She didn't give me her name but said dancing was her life—her absolute passion. It had been what she had lived for because it made her heart soar. She was dancing right there for me with the biggest smile on her face. I felt the passion so strongly I actually wanted to get up and dance to show everyone in the church how great she was. I could see that she was so happy that I felt her love of movement.

"How did you pass away?" I said tentatively.

Suddenly, everything went black. I was overwhelmed with the most dreadful cloak of desperation and foreboding. I knew for certain that this poor dancer had died instantly, which was bad enough, but the sadness and despair that she felt was just so agonizing. I burst into tears, crying in deep, rasping sobs. I couldn't help it. I didn't go back to the spiritual church after that. I had enough going on in my life without dealing with other people's issues. It may sound selfish, but there was a large element of self-preservation involved.

By this stage, I was surrounded by spirits all the time. They were forever butting into my life and making themselves known. It felt like it was getting out of control, although it was also quite funny sometimes. One time, Sonia and my brother John came to visit for a weekend. We were having a beer together in the living room and discussing spirits and paranormal activity as I tried to fill them in on what had been happening.

"I really don't believe in all of that," John said, a little dismissively. "I don't mind talking about it, but, well, really?"

I suppose this was a breakthrough of sorts because previously he hadn't wanted to hear anything of it. I knew then that the spirits were going to show him.

John had only had a couple of beers when he stood up and walked over to the dining room on the way to get another one. He stopped at the doorway and turned to face us as though he was about to say something. Suddenly, he moved abruptly to one side, as though he had been shoved. He looked surprised and disconcerted as he sought to balance himself. Then, just as he managed to do so, he was apparently shoved again. The look on his face was priceless. John looked in complete shock. I knew it was a spirit doing it, but he denied it vehemently. Mind you, he still looked white as a sheet and completely shocked even ten minutes later.

"Nothing happened," he insisted. "I just lost my balance. That's all."

I couldn't help giggling. I knew exactly what had happened.

Even so, the incident with the dancing girl affected me profoundly, and I kept thinking about it. I realized it had sealed what I already knew. I needed to step away from the spiritual world for a time. I just wasn't ready for whatever it was trying to tell me. I called my, by now, good friend Pam, the Reiki practitioner, and asked for her advice.

"I think I really need to get all these spirits out of the house," I told her. "It is time."

Pam understood completely and said she would speak with her friend Sri, who knew about house cleansing. Within minutes, she came back to me and said she and Sri would come over the next day.

Over the course of a few hours, the two of them managed to cleanse the house, placing crystals around, taping up mirrors and any glass, and burning sage. It looked like something out of a paranormal or poltergeist movie. In fact, my life had become very much like one of those movies. The following day the energy in the house felt markedly better. It was as though a weight had been lifted. I already knew that all paranormal activity would stop, and it did.

I had mixed feelings for a few moments. I had always been spiritually aware, even as a young girl. If this was to be the end of my connection with the spirit world, that would be quite a loss. However, it would also be quite nice to live somewhere with normal, relaxed energy for a while. The past few months had been pretty manic.

I decided that the best tonic of all would be to take some me time. I had been so keen to fill my days with meaningful activities and been so absorbed by my brush with spirits, I had often forgotten to give myself the space I needed to acknowledge my emotions on losing Rick. Recovery from what I had been through was centered on awareness. As long as I was aware of how I was feeling and not suppressing it, I would be okay.

Chapter 8

▬ ▬ ▬ ▬ ▬ ▬ ▬ ▬ ▬ ▬ ▬ ▬ ▬

A NEW WAY OF LIVING

If I had worried that Pam and Sri's efforts had severed my connection to the spirit world, I was shortly to be proven very wrong. In fact, as I was to discover, the link only became stronger.

Whoever, or whatever, was my permanent guide, was constantly pushing me on to try new things. My thirst for knowledge was almost insatiable. My guide clearly didn't want the grass to grow under my feet, though, because I had no sooner finished the counseling and Spanish courses before I was propelled toward not just one but two more challenging activities.

The first was a course in day trading, where people are taught how to buy and sell stocks and shares on a day-to-day basis. I had always been hugely interested in the stock markets. I had previously bought oil shares on numerous occasions but never had experience in spread betting. I never once believed I had anything like the skill or knowledge to even consider speculating myself. Nevertheless, my inner voice all but insisted I book myself on a course, and so that was exactly what I did. I wasn't too bad at it either. In fact, if I do say so myself, I think I had a bit of a knack at picking buy or sell trades that would allow me a profit. It almost felt intuitive. Perhaps my guide was lending a hand. Fortunately, there are no stock market rules on getting tips from the spirit world. I never made a fortune, but I certainly didn't lose anything either.

The second course I was directed toward was Reiki training. Again, this was something I would never have envisaged myself doing. Having conquered my fears and signed up for the introductory course, I found I loved it. In fact, the training left me buzzing and eager to explore it more. I didn't need any guidance or suggestion to go straight back in and sign up for further training for the next level, which worked toward a Reiki master's qualification.

I became almost used to the unseen nudges I'd frequently receive. I certainly didn't fear them. In fact, I listened hard for them now because every time they were uncannily just right. I now knew from experience that if I didn't get it, or somehow ignored a clear suggestion, it would invariably happen again a second time. This repeat was always a little more urgent, and I always felt a little apologetic that I hadn't been in tune enough in the first place. If something was suggested twice, I would always immediately follow through. After all, my guides had never let me down before.

This was how I came to read the book called *The Celestine Prophecy* by James Redfield.[1] I think I had misheard my guide the first time because I wasn't quite sure it was the book for me, but I was glad to be given a second, firmer nudge. The book, which uses ancient Peruvian wisdom to explain how to make connections between this world and what is happening right now and how it relates to our futures, was truly inspiring. It confirmed to me that everything I was experiencing was normal as I went through my spiritual awakening.

I never really needed confirmation as such, but it would have been very easy to keep telling myself that I was making it up or was looking for something that wasn't there to fill the huge gap in my life created by Rick's passing. I know when I spoke to people about this side of my life, some were skeptical. They were polite, of course,

---

[1] James Redfield, *The Celestine Prophecy* (London, Bantam, 1994).

but I sensed they were thinking that my spiritual awakening was just a phase brought on by the early stages of intense grief. They were right to some extent, I suppose. In most cases, a spiritual awakening is brought on by some sort of trauma.

A few would come right out and say as much: "Oh, it is just the grief." (Subtext: You're just wishing for some answers to the unanswerable. It'll all go back to normal in time.)

Even though I felt comfortable with what was happening to me, *Celestine Prophecy* settled my mind. One of its big messages was to look from the soul, not the mind. If we see things too much in black and white, it is easy to miss the true picture. We all need to open ourselves up to the possibility that we live in a deeply mysterious world, filled with sudden coincidences and synchronistic encounters that seem destined, if we'd only but accept it.

As I read about soul connections and how when we are inexplicably drawn to complete strangers there is, in fact, an explanation, I thought about Simon. I had never experienced anything like what had happened on the plane that day and then again when I saw him at the business event. There was such a deep, powerful energy between us it was almost overwhelming. Just being close to him sent my soul into a whirlwind of emotion.

A soul connection is eternal; within it there lies an unconditional love. It's a spiritual love that far surpasses any love that we feel in our normal 3-D lives. Of course, we love our parents, children, partners, and friends very much, but more often than not, we are not bonded at the level of the soul. We say we love them unconditionally, but in reality, we love them with conditions.

I hadn't seen Simon or spoken to him since the second time we met but felt compelled to keep the link alive by reading his social media posts. The extraordinary thing was that when I read them, I always understood his exact mood when he wrote them. From just a couple of words, I knew exactly what sort of day he'd had, what he was feeling, and whether he was happy or sad. It was the strangest feeling I had ever had. This sensation of inner knowing was so strong and unusual, yet utterly amazing. Of course, I had heard of the term *soul mates* before, but I'd never given the true meaning behind the concept much thought. To be perfectly honest, if somebody had described to me what I am describing before I had experienced this myself, I wouldn't have believed it. The idea that it would ever be possible to have such a connection with someone I didn't know would have sounded far too romantic and far-fetched for me to digest.

After I finished reading the book, I felt compelled to see Simon again. I couldn't seem to stop myself.

I sent him a message asking him if he'd like to meet up and received one in return almost straight away saying something to the equivalent of, "Sounds good. When?"

A meet was fixed for the following week. I was really excited. I felt at last we were on our way to finding out what it was between us. It wasn't that I was looking for a relationship—far from it, in fact. I was still a long, long way from even contemplating ever giving myself up to a man again. I just valued the deep connection we had and felt intuitively that this person was going to be an important part of my life. I needed to find out what that part would be.

Then, just twenty-four hours before we were due to meet, I received a short text. Simon couldn't make it, blaming something coming up at work.

Even as I read it, I knew it was nothing to do with work. There was another reason he had called it off. I sensed fear. *But why would he be afraid?* I wondered.

I sent an upbeat reply, telling him not to worry and suggesting we meet up another time. The date was duly put in our respective diaries, and I looked forward to it with the same anticipation as before.

As the next time drew close, I discerned that Simon was feeling hesitant and concerned. There was an overwhelming sense of inner conflict. He wanted to but didn't want to. Sure enough, a few days later, he canceled again.

This could carry on forever, I thought. Simon was clearly conflicted. I couldn't blame him. I didn't fully understand the strength of our connection either, but at least I had some insight into it thanks to my guides. I certainly didn't fear it.

I decided to attend another of Simon's business courses, telling myself once more that it would be useful for my various commercial activities. I had recently bought my first property, a small apartment in Surrey, which was hopefully the beginning of a buy-to-rent, or holiday rental, business. Funnily enough, it was something I had talked about with Rick a couple of years earlier when we discussed what I would do when I eventually went back to work. We'd agreed that becoming a landlord was the perfect profession for me. I'd bought the property just before Christmas, rented it out almost immediately, and was already thinking of buying another.

I was, of course, lying to myself by thinking I only needed advice on growing my business by attending Simon's course. I just needed to see him. I needed to figure out what was going on between us.

I booked tickets to the event and counted the days. I had cold feet once or twice but knew I had to be the one to break the impasse and meet Simon face-to-face.

When the day itself came, I felt surprisingly nervous. I wasn't quite sure what to expect with Simon blowing so hot and cold on our meetings. I wondered how he would behave.

As it was, he chose the easy option, which was to pretend that nothing had happened. He singled me out to say hello and thank me for coming, but that was as far as it went.

The actual conference continued on much the same vein. Mercifully, he didn't pull me to my feet to repeat the airplane story again, but he looked in my direction a great deal as he spoke. In fact, for much of the event, it felt like I was the only one there—the only one that counted anyhow.

Once it ended, there was little opportunity to say goodbye or have any sort of meaningful conversation because he was once more surrounded by people asking questions, so I went on my way. I felt quite disappointed. I needed answers and to fully understand what our connection was all about. The only way to get them would be to speak openly and honestly with Simon, yet he seemed to be doing everything in his power to avoid this. As I began the drive home, I resolved to leave Simon to it. It was perfectly understandable that he feared what he (and I) didn't understand, and there was no good to come out of forcing the issue. I would just have to continue my research on my own accord and see what I could find out by myself.

As I drove, I ran through the what-next options in my head. Meditation seemed like an obvious answer for sure. In fact, meditation was to become a big part of my life in the weeks that followed. It was a skill that needed to be learned, like so many of the things I was doing now, but setting aside time for reflection was so rewarding. It was also the perfect way to ask and receive answers through my channeling.

I smiled to myself as I remembered one particular recent meditation. Feeling somewhat frivolous, I asked a less-than-specific question of my spirit guide.

"Do you have any messages for me?"

Almost immediately, I saw Rick sitting behind a desk, writing intently. He looked up and smiled and then got to his feet. I caught my breath as he walked slowly toward me. It was always so lovely to see him again. As he walked, he picked up a book from the corner of the desk. It was a small book, a paperback novel I think. Once he reached a position of less than half a meter away, he held out the book, fanning the pages from one end to the other. I understood immediately what he was telling me.

"You want me to write a book of my own?" I said.

He smiled, and I nodded to show I understood.

"Is there anything else I need to know?" I asked tentatively.

I was never sure how much I should ask, or whether I should let him take the lead.

One red rose and a handful of balloons appeared from nowhere, and Rick presented them to me.

"It's not my birthday, but thank you," I giggled.

I loved seeing Rick in this way. Yes, I had lost my husband's physical body, but his spirit was, without a doubt, still with us. It comforted me and gave me pleasure like nothing else on earth.

Even so, I was somewhat bewildered by what his gift meant. I adored expressions of love like this but felt sure there was more to it than that. I reminded myself to be patient because the answer would come. It always did.

I was right too. Later in the day a letter had arrived congratulating me for passing my counseling exam. Late that evening, I received a note from my brother Stephen to say well done. And the picture on the front of the note? Balloons. They were almost identical to the ones Rick had given me. My husband had been the first in line to congratulate me—how very thoughtful.

So, meditation was definitely high on my list when it came to the search for answers. As I continued my drive back from Simon's event, I pondered what else I could do. I was still receiving plenty of messages through telepathy and dreams. All the same, though, the messages were not particularly targeted at anything I thought I needed to know. If I wanted to get answers, I needed to ask questions.

I thought about automatic writing again. Perhaps now that I understood so much more, I could channel my messages a bit better. I'd be able to protect myself from any of the less pleasant elements of this tool of communication. I'd spoken to a few people who were knowledgeable about such things, and they had all said it was crucial that it was done in the right circumstances. I'd been advised to think very carefully about how I went about it. I should, I was told, light a candle, say a small prayer for protection, and play some pleasant soft music before beginning my writing. I certainly felt convinced enough to give it a go, so I sat down and started to write.

This time it was very different. A spirit was not writing through me anymore; it was telepathic. I was taken aback by the information I received. The love that I felt through these messages was so overwhelming. I had never felt such love. It was a wonderful connection. Who was sending these messages with such love? I was guided to write acres of beautiful poetry that was filled with so many messages about how everyone in the world should be living through love. Even so, my brain was still flooded with questions and very few answers.

Maybe I just need a bit of a break, I thought. Luckily, I was off to Portugal shortly to celebrate my mother's eighty-second birthday along with my sister Jackie. We would be visiting Sonia, as she had not long before decided to move to Portugal full time, so it would be a wonderful time to enjoy us all together. I would take the time to recharge my batteries and tackle it all when I got back.

The holiday was amazing too. It was lovely to spend those carefree days with my mother and sisters, and I felt more relaxed than I had for a very long time. The four of us did very little other than soak up the sun, amble around a few sights, and eat and drink very well as we enjoyed each other's company. I'd almost forgotten how nice it could be to do and think about nothing.

Nevertheless, I did stick to my daily routine of meditation. It was only for fifteen minutes a day, and because I had gotten into the habit and it really helped me relax, I didn't want to stop now, especially as the messages I received were of such love. And, I have to admit, there is something quite special about meditating with the sun bathing your face. The natural warmth seems to fuel the energy around you.

As I lay there with my eyes closed on about the third or fourth day of our break, I had a sudden flash of inspiration. A question popped into my head that had never occurred to me before, and once I thought of it, it was so obvious that I was surprised I hadn't thought of it before.

I reached for pen and paper and wrote: "Who is channeling all these messages to me?"

I felt a powerful surge of love through my body. It was as though I had asked entirely the right thing at that moment.

"Angels of the light," came the answer.

Angels of the light, I thought. How lovely. I had no idea what it meant, but it just sounded so beautiful. And then I was prompted to draw a love heart. I had such a breathtaking feeling of calm at that moment it is hard to describe.

Once I had finished writing, I told Sonia and Jackie all about it.

"I have no idea what angels of the light are," I said, although clearly it had a very religious overtone.

The strange thing was, I had always been agnostic. It wasn't that I didn't want to know about religions or wasn't interested in them. In fact, I had read an English version of the Koran while living in the Middle East, along with the Holy Bible. My auntie was a Jehovah's Witness, and when I was younger, I would sit and read with her. However, I was adamant I wouldn't dedicate my life to something until it had shown itself.

"I will not dedicate my life to something I can't see or feel," I'd often said. "If He shows Himself, then I will dedicate the rest of my life to Him.'

Sonia felt broadly the same way, so I could see she was curious about my angels.

"Nothing else for it," she said, typing her password into her laptop. "Google is your friend."

I watched as she quickly pressed the keys, picking out the words *angels of the light*. She scrolled a little, clicked a link, and started reading, nodding to herself as she did so.

"Interesting, she murmured, still reading.

"What?" I said, trying not to sound impatient.

"God's messengers," she said, looking up from the laptop. "It says angels of the light are God's messengers."

I instantly burst into tears. I couldn't help it. Suddenly, so much seemed to make sense. The presence that had guided me for so many weeks had always felt so loving and generous of spirit. These messengers of God had been surrounding me and looking after me for all this time. I felt almost humbled to be so fortunate. Since Rick had passed away, I had felt something stroking my face or my hand on a regular basis, especially at times when I was feeling low. I knew it wasn't Rick, but I also knew whoever it was, they were full of love. I know knew they were my angels that had been walking alongside me, comforting me in my hour of need. This was the moment when I found my connection to God. It was such a huge leap forward in my clarity of thought that it almost made me dizzy. What was even more surprising was the day before while meditating I had a vision of angels on either side of me. I was surrounded by them. It was unimaginably beautiful.

Now that I'd asked the right questions, my hunger for information rose another notch. I was onto something, and it was incredible. It was my duty to understand my guides properly. Sure enough, my angels of the light stepped in again, and on the flight home, I was guided to write a short poem—the one you find at the front of this book. I was also prompted to read an article about an angel reader in a magazine I had in my bag. Apparently, a man named Kyle Gray understood so much more about the angels that surround us and could communicate with them. Best of all, he was available for readings over Skype. I wrote his details down and got in touch almost as soon as I got home.

"I'd really like to have a reading to see if you can offer me any more information," I said on his inquiry form.

To my pleasure, he agreed to speak with me the following day. When we did eventually face one another over Skype, I couldn't have been more surprised by his opening sentence.

"I am here to help with messages from your angels," Kyle said, "but you already have the ability to communicate with spirits."

I blinked back at him for a few moments, unsure of what to say.

"I'm just not sure I am asking the right things," I stammered. "I get a bit confused."

I smiled self-consciously and added, "I've not been doing this for long."

The angel reader smiled back. He had a nice feel about him and immediately put me at ease.

SAOIRSE BROWN

"Well, I can see your angels around you," he said, looking at the screen intently.

Inwardly, my heart soared. I knew it to be true, but it was nice to hear confirmation.

"They have a message for you," he went on. "They are sorry they weren't able to help with whatever issue you have had recently, but they were there with you."

I wondered what incident he meant, and then the answer came into my head. They were referring to the time when all those spirits invaded my home—the time when it all got to be a bit much, and I had to call upon Pam and Sri to come and help me clear them all out.

"Remember, you need to protect yourself," he explained. "Don't be afraid to call upon your guides and angels to help either."

I blushed a little. I have always been terrible about asking anyone for help.

I was advised to ground myself for things to become easier.

Everyone was reading my thoughts.

As we spoke, I began to understand a little more about what was happening around me. What I was experiencing now was a deep, overpowering spiritual love. Many people shun it because they can't understand or control it. Or they try to push it away by controlling one another, which is the source of so much conflict around the world. But there was no need for anyone to feel insecure or to try to disconnect themselves from such a sacred source of love. If we allow ourselves to be filled with such boundless, unlimited energy and love, we will be lifted into higher self-awareness.

As I ended the conversation with Kyle, I felt more love than I had ever experienced. The experience was so intense that I wanted everyone to feel it. I wanted to share it with the world and use it to make a difference. After all, this was surely why it had been given to me: to share this experience with others.

Somehow, I knew that I needed to be baptized. It seemed like the only sensible thing to do right then. The second I thought it, my mind was completely made up. I would not hesitate. I immediately made arrangements to travel to my mother's house, in my hometown of Scunthorpe in the north, to tell her of my decision.

"I want to do it too," she responded, much to my surprise.

Oddly, once I made my decision, a number of others said they'd like to do the same. By the time I telephoned to speak to the somewhat surprised reverend at my local church, I had a list of five people who wanted to be baptized: me, my mother Sheila, my daughter Ellie, my sister Sonia, and my niece Lindsay.

"It's probably going to take a bit of organizing because we are all from different parishes," I said apologetically.

"I would love to do it," the reverend said straight away. "It is not often I get the chance to bless three generations."

Everyone was amazing, and we somehow managed to get through all the complicated arrangements together. Even as we were working out the logistics, I kept thinking it was going to be a very emotional day. It was almost as though we were organizing a wedding, which, I suppose, in a way it was. We would be promising ourselves to God.

On the day itself, I felt almost sick with nerves and anticipation. My family all teased me as we walked into the church.

"This was your idea," Sonia said with a smile on her face. "You need to enjoy it."

"Come on, Mum," Ellie said, putting a protective arm around my shoulders.

I thought I would be able to hold it all together, but when the reverend asked me to explain the reason why I wanted to be baptized, the floodgates opened.

"It's the love I feel," I sobbed. "I wanted to share it. I need to help others."

The reverend nodded and smiled. "You have the Holy Spirit within you," he said gently. "I understand how you feel."

Later in the day, after the service had ended and I had fully calmed down, I asked the reverend what he had meant. I sensed he had more of a story to tell.

SAOIRSE BROWN

"I used to be an engineer," he began. "Then I felt the call to become a reverend. It was such a powerful feeling that I couldn't ignore it."

"You can't, can you?" I agreed.

It was good to know I was not the only one to be so overwhelmed by the spiritual pull.

All the same, I felt duty bound to apologize to the reverend's wife for being such a blubbering wreck throughout the service.

"It must have all seemed a bit silly, me warbling on about love in that way."

"Oh, not at all," she said, squeezing my arm. She had the same gentle charm as her husband. "He's just the same, you know," she added, nodding over at the reverend as she spoke. "He talks about the love that surrounds us all the time too. There are others who come to the church who say the same thing."

The reverend's wife paused, and I saw a wistful look flutter over her brow.

"It must be very beautiful," she said quietly. "I have yet to find it but am hopeful that it will come to me one day."

I hoped so too. I was only now beginning to realize what a blessing this awakening was.

Chapter 9

BELIEVE

It had now been nineteen months since Rick had passed, and although he wasn't with us physically, I still felt him around all the time, ushering me on to learn and serve my purpose. I had long since accepted that grief hits us all in different ways, and whatever well-wishers try to say, I don't believe you ever get over the death of a loved one. You just learn to live with it.

Without a doubt, grief changes you as a person. However, it doesn't need to define who you are. Everyone needs time to grieve and work through the stages of denial, anger, bargaining, depression, and acceptance. No one will ever go through all of these stages at the same pace or in the same way or even go through all of them. It is an entirely individual process that could take six months, maybe two years, or possibly ten years before someone starts living again. Sadly, in some cases and for some people, it never truly happens.

I never once shied away from talking about my grief. I knew that grief and whatever comes after it was something that I needed to talk about publicly to help others who were going through the same thing. I felt passionately about helping other people, so perhaps I would be able to save them from some of the pain and loss I had experienced. In following this path, I discovered something else very enlightening: the more you give, the more you get back.

I had sensed this for a while but hadn't really articulated it. It was only when I signed up for a public speaking course that all the thoughts that were jumbling around in my brain seemed to make a bit more sense.

I was somewhat surprised when I was guided toward enrolling on the course. Although I wasn't exactly shy, public speaking was far more Rick's cup of tea. He'd always liked nothing better than holding an audience—the larger, the better. The idea of me getting up on stage and delivering any sort of speech filled me with horror. Still, in among all the new things I was trying, I was firmly put in the direction of public speaking, so public speaking it was. I trusted what I was being guided to do, knowing that the meaning behind it would be revealed to me at some point soon.

I booked a place on a taster weekend with the Andy Harrington's Public Speaking University, which promised to teach me about how it was all done. The session was being held at a hotel near Gatwick. I had no idea what it would all be about, or even what I wanted to publicly speak about, but I was told that the purpose of the weekend was to dig deep to find the stories we would like to share with the world.

When I arrived, I was nervous and unsure, but the speaking coaches seemed to know instinctively what I needed to get me started.

"You should talk about what you are passionate about," they coaxed. "Your story—what you need to share with the world."

Of course, they were entirely right. I was living the story I wanted to share. Even though I was uncomfortable with the process of public speaking, this was a huge opportunity to help lots of people in my position. My story needed to be shared.

Once I had relaxed into the weekend, I really enjoyed it, despite my initial nerves. The coaches taught all the basics of what we would need, and by the time I went home, I felt that with a few more months of training, I would have all the tools to be able to tell my story on stage. As with all of the things I was trying, I couldn't leave it there. I then signed up for the full Monty: the entire public speaking course, which would run over a one-year period. I was assigned a speaking coach named Cheryl Chapman.

Interestingly, though, it was one thing that was said on that very first weekend that proved the most valuable. Andy Harrington, who ran the academy, did a presentation to everyone on the course that was essentially to motivate us all and urge us to speak because we all have the gift but just don't use it. To illustrate the point, he told a short story.

"A little boy goes downstairs on Christmas morning to open the gifts that are laid out under the tree," Andy began. "He is excited to see what had been left out for him. Yet, he is hugely disappointed when he begins to open them and realizes that he already has every gift he receives. Each one of the toys are the exact replicas to the ones he has upstairs in his bedroom. The boy turns to his mother who is watching him open his gifts and asks: 'Mummy, I already have these gifts. Why are they the same?'

"To which his mother replies: 'Yes, Son, but have you used those gifts? No new gifts will come until you start using the gifts you already have.'"

As he said it, it was like a penny dropping in my mind. Throughout my spiritual journey, I had been shown time and time again that this was true. Having a gift is not enough; it is using it and sharing it that is the important thing.

Each time I have learned a new skill, I have made sure that I have shared it with others. It can be as simple as passing someone in the street and saying a few words that person needs to hear or offering a stranger a couple of hours of my time for coaching or healing. I can see in the faces of those I help that they are touched and that I have made a difference in their lives. We have no idea what others are going through until we take the time to listen.

I understood immediately that I was being guided toward continuing to learn and share. Equally, I knew that when we trust this guidance, the universe just keeps on giving to us and opening up more opportunities. The more you give, the more you receive.

As if to reinforce the point, this was shown to me in a very real way during my next venture: a Reiki master's course that was being held in Glastonbury, Somerset, run by Torsten Lange of the Reiki Academy London. My interest in Reiki had continued at a pace over recent months, and I had recently added to my skill set with an online diploma in crystal healing, which I felt complimented my Reiki work nicely. I was right. The combination of crystals and Reiki worked beautifully together, and everyone I worked with seemed to go away very happy.

For the Reiki two course that I had completed before this master's course, I had been shown how to send distant healing to someone, whether they were in the next room or on the opposite side of the world. I had received Reiki like this myself a few months earlier, and it most definitely worked for me. Of course, I did wonder if it was all psychological. Was it just because I had been told it had been sent and that I should feel better, and therefore, I allowed my mind to believe it? It was good to find out myself how it worked. After I had worked on the theory, I gave distant healing a go.

I went into one room, while my client lay on a bed in another room. I pictured him lying down in front of me and started sending Reiki, beginning at the top of his head. When I arrived at his eyes, I felt a very irritating tickle in my throat that I just couldn't get rid of. I knew intuitively that he was suffering with some sort of eye irritation. My mind continued down the rest of his body, clearing chakras, and then pulled up abruptly at his stomach. My hands raised up, and once again, my intuition kicked in. It felt like I had just put an Alka Seltzer in a glass and the water had fizzed up explosively. I immediately knew my client was suffering from acid in his stomach. When I had finished, I went through to the other room to tell him what I had found through sending Reiki, and he confirmed he was indeed suffering with an infection in both eyes and that he was also suffering daily from acid in his stomach that had been diagnosed by a doctor. After that day, I questioned Reiki no more and was looking forward to continuing on to become a Reiki master at the Glastonbury course.

It was no coincidence that the course was being held in Glastonbury. The area has been well known since ancient times for being at the center of ley lines and powerful earth energies. Anyone with even the slightest tendency toward spirituality cannot help but be moved by the atmosphere in and around the city. The Reiki course was being held at the beautiful Abbey Retreat House, which features carvings of dragons said to indicate early knowledge of the earth dragon energies encircling the area.

The course was, as anticipated, incredible and took my learning to a new level. However, it is something that happened outside of the classroom that really sealed my lesson about the correlation between giving and receiving.

During our free time, we all did our utmost to experience as much as we could of the local area, following the well-worn spiritual trail to take in sites such as the crossing places of the ley lines at the abbey ruins and Glastonbury Tor and the White Spring. One of my final excursions was to the Chalice Well gardens. The tranquil gardens feature one of Britain's most ancient wells and a sanctuary in which you can experience quiet healing. Indeed, the water is reputed to possess powerful healing qualities.

I spent some time at the well with some of the other ladies from the master's course and felt a tremendous sense of calm and inner strength as I left. There was definitely something about the place. Before we headed back, I stopped at the gift shop to get a few souvenirs. I was just getting ready to pay when one of the others decided she absolutely had to take some of the well water home with her.

"I'm really sorry, but would you mind if I cut in line?" she said, touching my arm lightly. "I'm in a real rush now, but I really would like to take some well water with me."

She showed me an empty water bottle by way of explanation. They were selling these in the shop to allow you the benefit of taking some water home with you. She was obviously wanting to do just that.

"Of course." I smiled. "Go ahead."

She was just about to slip in ahead of me when the cashier shook her head.

"Really sorry," she grimaced, "but I had already started with this lady's shopping, and I can't stop this transaction to take a card payment."

She meant me.

"Oh, don't worry," I jumped in. "Just add the bottle to my order, and I'll pay. Otherwise, it will just get confusing."

The lady who wanted to collect the water thanked me profusely and scampered off with her plastic bottle to gather her well water. I was just wondering what this lady would be doing with this healing water when the cashier broke my train of thought.

"I haven't charged you for the water bottle," she said.

"No, please, add it." I smiled. "I am happy to pay for it."

"I know you are, and that's why I am not adding it." She smiled back.

How lovely was that?

A few days later something similar happened. I'd been waiting for a while for my date to cook at the homeless shelter, so I got in touch to see if they had forgotten about me. They hadn't, but the only day they had available in the near future was the following day. Of course, I agreed straight away, although even as I did so, I was wondering how I would be able to cook a meal big enough for twelve people on such short notice.

After giving it some thought, I decided to go to Cook, a shop in our local village that sells delicious, home-style, precooked frozen

SAOIRSE BROWN

food. After a short while browsing the freezers, I headed to the checkout, my arms laden with enough food for a main course and dessert for a dozen people.

"Gosh, this is a lot of food," the cashier commented. "Do you have a big family?"

"It's not for me." I smiled. "I'm cooking at the homeless shelter tomorrow, and I only just found out. This seemed like the most sensible solution."

The cashier nodded in approval, and soon we were chatting about charities and volunteer work as she scanned my meal.

"Okay," she said at last, tapping the screen in front of her after having put the final dessert through. "My boss offers a discount when it comes to this type of work, so, as you are paying for this yourself, I would like to give you 30 percent off."

I was a little lost for words. It was such an unexpected act of generosity.

"Thank you," I managed to stammer out at last.

"Not at all," she replied. "You are doing a wonderful job. In fact, please go and pick a meal for you and your family, free of charge."

"Oh no, I couldn't do that," I replied, feeling quite uncomfortable. It was extraordinarily kind for this shop to help the homeless, but it didn't seem fair that I should be rewarded.

"I insist," the cashier said firmly. "You give, and now it's time for you to take back."

I did go and pick up a pie for my family, as I could hardly refuse, and I don't think she would have let me out of the shop if I had. Even so, I did cry. I cried because I had yet again been shown proof that when we give without expecting anything in return, it does come back to us in more ways than we'd ever imagine.

As the months rolled by, I began to feel that I was gaining a greater understanding of the world around me and what it all meant. I certainly saw that living a life with a mindful approach made the grieving process much easier. By making a conscious effort to control my thoughts, I managed to pursue the healing process very well. I wouldn't allow any sort of mental movies to keep playing in my mind. No thoughts of: *I should have ...* or *why didn't I?* I never entertained personal challenges by questioning why: *if only this happened* or *if only that.* I recognized doing that was utter madness. I couldn't change the situation, so why torment myself with such questions? This is not to say that I wasn't still having days that were full of sadness about Rick not physically being around. I did. I just allowed the emotions that bubbled up inside me to come to the forefront. I acknowledged them, accepted them without any judgement, and then released them. I learned how to give myself compassion and to tell myself that it was okay to feel exactly as I did—just as I would do for a friend in the same position.

Although I fully accepted I was not alone in my journey of spiritualism, I had stopped speaking to many people about my happenings. Over time, I had learned who would return *the look* if I said anything. The look happened when the person I was speaking to was clearly wrestling with whether to say what they were thinking: *It is just the grief speaking. You'll stop thinking these things in time.* To begin with, I told them they were wrong and I was not going to change. Over time, I realized it was a lot easier to keep things to myself with some people even though I was sure to offer as much support as I could to anyone who needed it.

Others were totally open to hearing about my spiritual happenings. Sonia, in particular, was always receptive, and that was probably just as well, as all sorts of messages seemed to come through for her.

One Saturday evening, I had only just sat down to meditate when my guide decided to come through. This wasn't unusual; messages would come now and again just to let me know they were there with me. Sometimes they wanted me to know specific things, while other times they were a bit more lighthearted, even playful.

"Tell Sonia I like her blue shoes," my female guide said and then followed with, "Margie."

Odd, I thought, *but okay.*

So, the following day, I relayed the message to my sister in a phone call.

"I have a message for you. My guide likes your blue shoes. Does that mean anything?" I said.

I had no need to explain what I meant. Sonia had been with me every step of the way on this journey. Even so, she couldn't believe it this time.

"OMG!" she squealed. "I went out last night, and when I walked into the pub, my friend said she liked my blue shoes. I was wearing blue shoes!"

My sister did, however, add that she had no idea who Margie was. I was able to clear that mystery up a day later when I was out walking my dog. I often chatted with my fellow dog walkers, although I never knew any of their names. I never asked, as the conversations were normally short.

That morning, I had gotten into a conversation with another of the dog walkers who I had never seen before. Somehow, the conversation turned to grief and how to live a life after someone close has died. It turned out this lady had recently lost her brother, and once again, I did my best to pass on what I had learned and be as comforting as I could possibly be. As we put our dogs into the backs of our respective cars, I asked the lady's name.

"I feel compelled to ask you your name." I grinned.

"Margie." She smiled back. "It's Margie."

Another mystery solved.

I rather enjoyed my spiritual interventions. After a while, they never surprised me. They became a part of my day-to-day life. It was rather lovely to realize we are not alone and are being looked after from the other side. There were so many occasions when I had telepathic guidance to do certain things, and I was shown the consequence of not following through on that guidance or following my intuition.

On my daily dog walks, I was firmly told to watch my car keys. I followed this guidance carefully and even laughed a little to myself every day when I zipped up my jacket with the key in it. *Nothing has happened to my keys,* I thought. *Is my guide losing its touch?* Then, sure enough, one day the key wasn't in my pocket when I got back to the car. I had lost the key, just as it had been predicted. I mentioned it to a couple walking by, and they immediately said that they'd been speaking to another couple who had found a key. They had left it in a mobile coffee van just a little way away on the National Trust land. What are the chances of that being a coincidence? All of these people being in the right place and discussing the right thing at the right time. It was my key.

Everything I was learning about myself and the world around me now was given to me by my guides and angels. If I had thought that the Coke can moving around was to be the best thing that I would be shown, then I had been very mistaken. Spirits can show you anything they need you to see. I could never understand why certain people would turn up in my life. We would build good friendships, and then we'd both lose touch after a couple of months. I now believe I was being given these people to help me progress spiritually and for business. They took me where I needed to be. Something always seemed to lead on from these people. Sometimes it was a lesson for me to learn, while other times it was me who provided the lesson for the other person to learn.

Now I was growing in confidence, and the spirits were unafraid to help me question myself and my preconceptions. One time, I went to visit Sonia because we hadn't seen each other for a while and another odd thing happened. As she was talking, Sonia put her hand up to her face to brush away a hair, and I noticed that she had a band aid on her wedding finger. I wanted to ask her what she had done but didn't want to interrupt. I waited patiently for a few minutes while she finished what she was telling me, although I couldn't take my eyes off the band aid on her finger all the while she spoke. Finally, when she stopped speaking, I came out with it.

"What have you done to your finger?" I asked. "Why have you got a band aid on it?"

Sonia looked utterly perplexed.

"What do you mean?" she said, putting her left hand out on the arm of the sofa and wriggling her fingers. There, gleaming on her third finger, was a beautiful engagement ring!

We both burst out laughing.

"What the hell just happened?" I said through my giggles.

I was immediately guided to get a pen and some paper and channeled messages, which is something I don't normally do when I'm with other people.

"Do you see what you think you see?" I wrote.

I didn't entirely understand why this had happened, but I was not afraid. I knew I would be guided to the answer when the time was right. Around one week later, I was guided to read the book *The Disappearance of the Universe*.[2] On a few occasions after this, I have seen things disappear and reappear in front of me in a split second. Was it all an illusion? I had no idea, but the point is I was ready to find out and was content to be guided to do so.

The guides and angels that surrounded me were also very disapproving of my obsession with keeping my house immaculately clean. I had always been very tidy, but my OCD had gone into overdrive after Rick died. Everything had its place, and the floors had to meticulously cleaned every day. I was told by a spirit in no uncertain terms that this had to stop and that I needed more time for myself to be still and just be. It took a while to calm down, but as the months went by, I did learn. The angels, as always, were right. The silly things we obsess over are ridiculous. Our time and energy are much better spent elsewhere.

My life was clearly meant to embrace more fun. One sunny day, when driving through London, I stopped at traffic lights and looked over to see a woman on a motorbike next to me. *That's it,* I thought,

---

[2] Gary R. Renard, *The Disappearance of the Universe: Straight Talk about Illusions, Past Lives, Religion, Sex, Politics and the Miracles of Forgiveness* (Carlsbad, CA: Hay House, 2004).

I need to take my bike test. For the seven years we had lived in Doha, Rick had owned a couple of motorbikes, mainly Ducatis. I'd also had a passion for them, but as the children were small and the roads treacherous there, I'd said no way. Driving over there, let's just say felt rather dangerous. I hadn't even wanted to drive in Doha, but I did. Riding a motorbike seemed like a step too far. Nevertheless, I had promised Rick that when we moved back to the UK and the kids were older, I would take my test. So, the following month, just as I had promised, that is what I did. I swapped my cleaning bucket for a small 125cc motorbike (well, not exactly, but mentally), and it felt good.

Sometimes, I was surprised by how much I had changed. I had never been a big reader of books before. Rick and Ellie always had and loved nothing better than spending long afternoons browsing in book shops. I had always been content with a glossy magazine and would take myself off to the coffee shop and ask them to come and find me when they had finished browsing. They would always return to me with arms laden down with books. Now, though, I had become an avid book reader. I had a thirst for knowledge like no other. I even disconnected the television because I never felt the need to watch it. I very rarely watched it previously anyway, and neither did the kids. I only ever kept it for when Rick came to the UK. I must admit, though, the customer services operative at Sky TV seemed to struggle somewhat with the concept that the contract was being terminated because none of us watched television.

With greater understanding and acceptance, this was where my journey of self-love began. I had made the conscious decision that I wanted to feel whole again—to be happy and enjoy all that life had to offer. I also knew that was what Rick would have wanted for me and our children. I had a choice, and my choice was to find a life full of love, peace, and happiness, although sadly it would be without my husband in it.

Everything I know about spirituality has been shown to me through spirits, either through my writing, reading a book, or

Saoirse Brown

guidance to watch a movie via Netflix or to take a certain course that would help me progress spiritually. I had begun to allow life to flow through me rather than fighting everything. I trusted and I had faith that what I was receiving was for my highest good. It most certainly presented a new way of living. The more I allowed this to happen, the more things aligned as if everything was being perfectly orchestrated. My life was becoming one big synchronistic event. I would put questions out to the universe about anything I needed to know, and the answer would come—either through a book or something I saw on social media or a sign in one way or another or maybe even just a comment someone made.

Everything about my life had changed now, even my walks with the dog. I had always loved nature, but now I felt more connected with it. On one very early morning walk, a deer ran out in front of me but then stopped and just stared right at me, as if it wanted to communicate. As it did so, I saw spirit energy beside me. It brought me to tears it was so beautiful. As time went on, I felt increasingly connected to all that there is. It is hard to explain with words what this feels like. It's a feeling of unconditional love. It is difficult to articulate, but the feeling is just so overwhelmingly powerful.

My desire to connect with who I really was began growing stronger and stronger, and I knew this would mean digging deeper into myself to find the answers. I continued with my meditation but was also guided to try yoga. I had always been curious about yoga but had put off trying. Following my guides' lead, I booked myself into a class at the gym where I was a member.

I was a little nervous of what to expect as I walked into the class. I really was a novice and rather hoped they weren't going to try to make me do anything to complex. I didn't think I was quite up to a full lotus pose. On entering the class, I noticed a balloon tied up on one of the ballet barres that circled the walls of the studio. Around fifteen minutes into the lesson, as we were all seated on the floor cross-legged in a sukhasana (easy pose), I looked up to see the balloon hovering above my head. Everyone laughed at the strange occurrence, and the instructor walked over to me smiling and asked me if it was my birthday. The words had barely left her lips before the balloon just dropped to my feet and lay on the wooden floor in front of me. How funny.

"No," I replied, giggling a little. "I'm being congratulated for coming here today. It has taken me months to get here!"

I did like it that the angels that surrounded me had a sense of humor. I loved the yoga too. Afterward, it felt as though I'd had a full-body massage. It was a lovely form of exercise, and I resolved to continue on with it regularly.

SAOIRSE BROWN

Chapter 10

▬ ▬ ▬ ▬ ▬ ▬ ▬ ▬ ▬ ▬ ▬ ▬ ▬

FREEDOM

Without a doubt, I was making progress thanks to my spiritual awakening. I was now completely confident that life centered around the lessons it taught us. Once a lesson had been learned or a test passed, we are free to move onto the next one.

Yet, I was aware that there was one lesson in my life I had not concluded. The learning from my connection with Simon was still very much open, and it hung over me like an unfinished book. It didn't matter how busy I was researching soul connections and how they worked; the thought that I had not resolved this thing, whatever this thing was, niggled at me constantly. Ever since that meeting on the plane, I had been desperate to know what it all meant but somehow completely unable to find any answers.

It was not for lack of trying. By now, I'd been to a number of his presentations, offered to meet up on numerous occasions, and spoken via messenger with him a few times. Simon was always friendly and attentive, pleased to hear from me, and definitely seemed to sense the connection too, although he'd never articulate it. Yet each time we ever got close to having a serious conversation or meeting up, he'd put on the brakes, and we'd be back to square one.

Nevertheless, I was keen for answers and was beginning to find it a little frustrating. I suspect that is why, during our next digital conversation, I chose to take a perfectly innocent comment made by Simon and accuse him of being judgmental.

"You're being very judgmental," I wrote accusingly.

Okay, not very combative, but taken in context it rather changed the tone of the conversation. Simon responded (quite curtly) that he had never judged me.

I then launched into a long and passionate rant about how I found the way he spoke to be judgmental.

Nothing. Complete radio silence. I was still no closer to working out the connection between us. If anything, I was probably further away.

My guides, once again, obviously decided to intervene, and I was guided to attend Simon's next event. I always responded to whatever I was guided to do, but I confess that I was a little reluctant this time. I'd been to these events on a few occasions that I pretty much knew the material by heart. Hell, with my newfound public speaking expertise, I could have gotten up on stage and made a pretty good fist of delivering the talk myself. Never mind, I was being told to go, so I booked my ticket. I might add that this time I didn't even tell Sonia I was going. She'd have thought I was going mad—or taking up a new career as a full-time stalker.

I drove to the event, took my seat, and waited. Simon entered the room, said a very cheery hello to me, and then perpetually looked over in my direction throughout the presentation just as he did each time.

Then nothing.

Yet again, I drove home frustrated and confused about what on earth it all meant. I couldn't understand why I had been guided to go because I still had no answers. As I sped along the road toward my house I kept asking myself: *Why?*

Then it came to me: judgment. I'd been completely wrong with my earlier accusation. Simon wasn't judging *me*. I was judging *him*.

In fact, I had been judging him and second-guessing him since we'd first met. No wonder I was not getting a clear view of our connection. I had to release my judgmental side and open my mind to know what was going on.

When I got home, I fired off a quick message to Simon: "It was lovely to see you today, and I feel I need to be honest. It wasn't you being judgmental. It was me!"

I pressed send and waited for the reply. To my relief, it came back almost immediately. Simon's response was frustratingly anodyne, saying it was lovely to see me. Nothing else.

That was more frustrating than ever. He refused to be drawn into any further conversation either, although this time I deliberately didn't push it.

I had begun to wonder if this was the end of it, and the lesson I needed to learn had been learned when I sensed I was being guided to attend another event, now when I say guided I actually mean pushed! By this time, I was beginning to become very reluctant indeed to go to yet another presentation, particularly so soon after the last one. Each one was exactly the same. Still, with a strong pull to go, I messaged Simon and told him I would be there again.

Strangely, by the time we reached the week leading up to the event, my ticket had still not arrived. I had never had an issue before with a ticket not being received. Not to be put off, I sent over a cheery reminder.

"Hey, you forgotten about me? I haven't received my ticket yet," I wrote.

Simon took a while to respond, but I was quite taken aback when he did finally come back to me.

He said I should get in touch with his office to arrange it!

The message sounded so abrupt and formal. It was certainly 180 degrees from our previous exchanges. As I stared at the phone in my hand, I became quite cross.

"I don't think so," I typed angrily. "I won't be chasing around for a ticket. I won't be attending."

Then I pressed send before I could change my mind.

I looked down at the screen to see his reply, which came back almost immediately. Two words: "your loss."

I did my best to put it all to the back of my mind.

Except I couldn't. I still didn't understand my lesson. I'd been guided to go to this event and then abruptly rebuked. What had that shown me? I started to analyze my behavior regarding the ticket, and it came to me. Ego. It was my pride and ego that was stopping me from going.

If I had lived through my heart and listened to my feelings, I would have been there. That was my lesson.

I thought of other times throughout the years when I had allowed my ego to run the show and realized it almost always left me in a less desirable situation. Why did I let my ego take over? I very quickly made the decision that this wasn't the way I wished to behave and made the switch from being guided by my ego to being led by my heart. Yes, it makes you vulnerable when you live and speak with an open heart, but it also opens you up to experiences that are so much more intense and important.

I decided not to pursue that particular event and let the lesson settle for a while. I wasn't sure if I needed to see Simon, and he seemed to have made it clear he wasn't all that keen on me for the moment either. We didn't communicate at all for a few weeks.

A fortnight later, I was packing my case, getting ready to be on my way to see family in the north, when I suddenly had an overwhelming feeling that I needed to attend Simon's upcoming event. *What's going on?* I thought, questioning this guidance. My guide pushed back. Through telepathy and synchronistic events that happened throughout the day, I was firmly being told to rethink my plans and go to the event. By the time I got into my car and started heading north, the feeling became very strong indeed.

I'm not going, I thought, unconsciously pressing the accelerator pedal a little harder and picking up my speed as though to emphasize my intentions to fulfill my original plan of completing my journey to the north.

Go to the event, was the unequivocal message I received in return. *You need to go.*

I knew then I had to listen. After all, the spirits had served me well so far. It was time to put my trust in the guidance once again. I returned home, unpacked my suitcase, and made some calls to cancel my trip up north. I realized it was becoming somewhat of a game, and I looked forward to what I would learn from this next meeting with Simon. *What would happen this time?*

The event was being held the following day, and this time I gave Simon no forewarning that I would be attending. I simply headed over to the venue and collected my wristband at the door.

I held my breath as it was signaled the event was about to begin. Simon had entered the hall from the back of the room, behind where I was sitting and began to walk up the aisle, greeting the delegates as he did so. If we followed our now well-worn routine, he would get to the place where I was seated and stop. He'd then make eye contact and hold it, just long enough so that it was over and above that of social norms, indicating something that neither of us seemed to be able to get to the bottom of. He was just a few feet away now, and I could clearly hear him welcoming someone in the aisle behind. He stopped talking and was about to take the next step, and out of nowhere, I felt compelled to keep my head down. Bowing my head, I looked at my feet and then stole a sideways glance at his feet. I saw him hesitate and then walk briskly on. The spell was broken.

I had no idea what exactly happened and perhaps never will, but I simply had to avoid eye contact. At that moment, I finally realized that there was no longer any attachment between us, and nothing hinged on the outcome of this connection. Instinctively, I no longer needed confirmation from him of what this was all about.

I already knew.

I had learned detachment. Since I had begun to trust everything I had been shown through my guides, I realized that detachment was the final lesson I would learn from this encounter with Simon.

I glanced over at Simon as he turned to address the crowd. Our eyes met for the last time. I gave him the slightest trace of a nod of recognition and got up to quietly leave the room. There would be no need for me to return to any more events. What needed to be done had been done.

Since my husband's death, I'd not only had to deal with the grief but also my spiritual awakening. That awakening had brought me much enlightenment but had been painful in many ways too. Although my psychic abilities had opened up before I had met Simon, my meeting him it had accelerated everything. He was my introduction to this new universe. Even though I didn't know it then and it took me months to work out, he had played a crucial role.

Simon was the chosen one to open the door to my spiritual journey because he was my soul mate. Some call it a twin flame, although I never really needed a title for it. The term *soul mate* is often misunderstood or misused. People often think it is a deep romantic bond with a life partner, often based on a physical attraction; for some people, that is the case, but this is not for everyone. The soul connection is something you have no control over. It's not something you decide. Simon was sent to challenge me and awaken my soul, stirring things deep within me that I didn't know existed. It wasn't a romantic connection—it was far more than that. He was the conduit to help me transcend to a higher level of consciousness and awareness. He had been instrumental in so many of the lessons I had learned. Now, though, it was time to go our separate ways.

I was so grateful to Simon for all of the beautiful things he had helped me experience throughout this difficult time. He had mirrored everything I needed to see in myself, bringing it to the surface so that I could better deal with what was happening around me. He helped me become a better person.

Even though we never discussed it, and in fact, Simon had stoically gone out of his way not to talk about the connection, I also know that meeting me brought issues to the fore for him. He never said so, but I just know. I would like to think that maybe one day we will be able meet again and discuss this special connection. It is difficult to understand why, when you have this strong bond, you can't be friends, or even lovers, but normally, for one of the two, it is too overwhelming and that person becomes a runner through fear. This type of love never goes away, though. People reunite after many years apart, and the love is still as strong. However, I will leave this one up to the universe. It always makes the right decisions. I know it has my back.

As I reflected on what had happened with Simon, I kept coming back to what the reverend had said during my baptism: "The Holy Spirit is within you." I'll admit, it had not made a lot of sense to me then. But I know knew, without a shadow of a doubt, that not only was I guided by spirit but I also have spirit that works through me. I have complete faith, trust, and belief that whatever I am guided to do is for the best interest of not just me but also for me to help others.

To quote from the Bible: "I will give you a new heart and put a new spirit in you; I will remove from you your heart of stone and give you a heart of flesh." (Ezekiel 36:26 NIV)

This verse will always resonate with me. I didn't find it in the Bible. It has just popped up on a couple of occasions when I have needed to understand a little more. He removes from us a heart of stone that rebels against God and puts into us a new heart that trusts God and follows his ways. It is a gift to be born again. This new birth is not caused by faith; the faith is caused by the new birth.

With each new day, things became clearer. I had now completely placed my faith in my spirit guides and the lessons I was constantly being shown.

Not long after the event with Simon that never was, I went to lunch with Ellie, Jack, and his Irish girlfriend, Freya. We were at a nice restaurant in Guildford, and I felt more relaxed than I had been in a while as the conversation ebbed and flowed. It was lovely to see both my children look so happy after all they had been through losing their beloved father. We were very blessed to have each other.

For some reason, the conversation came around to the differences between Irish and English names and the sometimes incomprehensible spellings of Irish names—well, to us anyhow.

"The one I always like is S-A-O-I-R-S-E," Ellie said, spelling it out letter by letter. "When you say it, it sounds like Seersha."

"What a beautiful name," I said immediately. "I absolutely love it."

As the conversation carried on, all I could think about was the name Saoirse. What did it mean? I instinctively felt that that name was for me and whatever it did mean would resonate with me.

Out of nowhere, a thought popped into my head: *I am going to change my name to Saoirse.* As odd as it sounds, it felt like God was giving me this name. Throughout the months of my automatic writing, I had been told on so many occasions that I was now free. Wouldn't it be the ultimate expression of that freedom to change my name? I had never felt so free internally than I had in the past weeks, so it seemed to make perfect sense.

As always, I looked out for spiritual confirmation I was on the right track. It seemed that today, my guide was communicating via synchronicities to show me that I was correct. By this time, my daughter and I had left the restaurant and were walking up High Street.

"Ellie, I think I need to change my name to Saoirse. I like it with my maiden name 'Brown'. I could change both. What do you think?" I said tentatively.

"Yeah, if you want to, why not?" was her response.

I was just about to talk a little more about it and explain my reasonings why when we both saw a priest walk past us with a huge cross around his neck. We both looked at each other, knowing we were thinking the same thing and laughed.

"Mum, you need to change your name." Ellie said, completely definitively this time.

Synchronicity number one.

The following morning, I was on the phone with a friend named Paul when we got into a conversation about God. Almost immediately, he said that when he had found God during a very difficult time in his life, he had been given a new name: David. I hadn't even mentioned my thoughts about the name change the day before.

Synchronicity number two.

After I finished our call, I logged on to my computer to Google the name Saoirse. Unable to resist, I opened up Facebook first to see what was going on. The top two posts on my Facebook newsfeed were about people who had changed their names.

Synchronicity number three.

Feeling certain now I was onto the right track, I keyed the name Saoirse into Google, and there is was at the top of the page: Saoirse = freedom. I think deep down I had always known. If there had ever been a scintilla of doubt, which there hadn't been, all trace had evaporated. My faith and trust in my guidance, as always, was rock solid.

There was more to come, though.

About a week later, I was at home sorting out some paperwork when the doorbell rang. Ellie was upstairs and Jack was out, so I went to open it. As soon as the door swung wide, I saw there were two men standing there with a woman. They were all young, smartly dressed, and seemed very friendly.

"Good morning. We are from the Church of God. Would it be okay if we read a couple of chapters from the Bible to you?" said one of the young men.

In the five years I had lived at the house, this was the first time anyone from the church had ever knocked at my door. Even so, I didn't for one moment consider turning them away.

"Of course, please come in," I replied.

I showed them into the kitchen, as my living room was upside down because I had employed decorators to freshen up the place.

"Do you have a religion?" the first young man asked politely.

"No, no I don't," I replied. "I'm spiritual."

They all nodded and seemed fine with my answer.

"And have you heard of the Church of God before?" pressed the other man.

"I'm afraid I haven't," I answered truthfully.

Again, the trio didn't seem too fazed by the response and asked my permission to show a short film to explain who they were. In no time at all, an iPad was produced, and I was watching a presentation about the Church of God, which was a Pentecostal Christian organization.

After this, the woman, who had not said much up until this point, did a reading from the Bible. I listened politely and nodded in agreement at some of the teachings. Obviously encouraged, the first man asked if I would be interested in attending their church.

"I don't normally attend church, as I have all that I need within me," I said. To be honest, I was waiting for the request for donations, but it never came.

Sensing a look of disappointment cast a shadow across their faces, I quickly followed up by patting my heart to explain I meant my spiritual beliefs and that God was within me.

The first man who had spoken at the door, who really stood out from the three because of his angelic good looks, nodded in understanding.

"Do you know how much it says in the Bible about the Holy Spirit?" he asked. "Would you like for us to come back next week and read for you?"

I thought about it and smiled. "I think it would be a lovely idea, but I should say I won't be able to do this on a regular basis."

The visitors looked very pleased. They gave me an exact date and time for their proposed visit the following week, and I reciprocated by handing over my telephone number. They all left shortly after that and said they were very much looking forward to seeing me again.

Later in the day, when Ellie came downstairs, I told her what had happened and how nice it had been talking to the three people from the Church of God.

"I said they could come back next week," I said. "You might like to sit in on the reading too. I found it quite interesting."

"Okay," Ellie said with a shrug.

I sensed she was hiding something, or perhaps was not keen on the idea, but I couldn't quite lay my finger on what was causing her an issue.

The following week, I arranged the lounge for my expected guests and made sure we had some nice biscuits in and that the kettle was filled in preparation. Then I sat down and waited at the appointed time. And waited. And waited.

Nothing.

Ellie popped downstairs to see if they had arrived and looked pointedly at her watch.

"I know," I said, making a face. "It seems so strange that they said they'd come and then just didn't show up. They had my telephone number, so they could have called if it was inconvenient for whatever reason."

Ellie looked like she wanted to say something, so I stayed silent.

"Mum, I wanted to say something last week," she said at last. "But that day you said they were here, well, I never heard anyone downstairs. Not a peep."

I looked over at her, disbelievingly.

"But I gave them my business card," I said emphatically. "They were definitely here last week, Ellie!"

I felt very confused. Perhaps it was a test of my faith. A few years before I would have almost certainly have turned them away from my doorstep. This time, though, with my new enlightenment, I had welcomed them into my home. Had I passed the test? What was the purpose of it? One thing was certain: the trio never came back, whoever they were.

I mentioned this to my friend Sri the next time I saw him. He laughed and asked me if I had heard of ascended masters visiting people to test their faith.

"Well, yes I have," I replied thoughtfully. "But why on earth would they want to visit me?"

We both laughed. My world was becoming one mysterious, magical, synchronistic event, and I was really enjoying playing the game.

Chapter 11

■ ■ ■ ■ ■ ■ ■ ■ ■ ■ ■ ■ ■ ■ ■ ■

THE BIGGEST TEST OF ALL

Without a doubt, Rick was still constantly making his presence felt. Wherever Jack, Ellie, and I looked, there were signs to show he was still around us. Some were very subtle and others hilariously funny, but nonetheless, they were still there. Even Jack's girlfriend, Freya, got an introduction even though she'd never had the opportunity to meet him.

Freya had come over from Ireland to celebrate her birthday, and she and Jack spent a day and a night in London. They'd done all the usual tourist stuff, visiting hot spots like Buckingham Palace, the Tower of London, and a few museums, and then returned to their hotel to freshen up before going out to dinner. Freya was quite taken aback when she went to the wardrobe to take out a dressing gown and found the name Richard Haworth on the tab inside. It was the designer's name, but having previously been alerted to my husband's tendency to pop up in the strangest places, Freya immediately took it as a sign.

The odd excursion to London notwithstanding, Rick's most frequent appearances were in and around our home. Not long after the incident with the dressing gown, I was at home catching up with emails from friends when I heard a scratching at the door at around

133

eleven o'clock at night. I was immediately alert, panicking that I had accidently left the dog out in the garden. I raced to the door and pulled it open to see that no one was there. I stepped out into the garden in case she'd wandered off but couldn't see her anywhere. Then, as I turned to go back in, I saw her through the window. She was curled up fast asleep on a chair in the living room.

How odd, I thought. *Perhaps it was a bird.*

I'd barely returned to my chair in front of my computer when I heard the same scratching. I went back to the door, opened it, and, once again, there was nothing there. Shaking my head, I started back to my former position, deciding to send a text message to Sonia to tell her about what was happening. I picked my phone up from the side table where I had left it as I went past and glanced at the computer screen to check the time. The large clock read 11:11, and then, for no reason whatsoever, the computer shut itself down and promptly started up again. I clicked my phone on, and there in glorious color, was a photo of Rick. It wasn't a screen saver. It was one I hadn't seen for years. He was looking relaxed and happy, staring at the screen with a big grin on his face.

"Well hello to you," I said out loud. "You certainly know how to get my attention!"

I already knew that it was no coincidence that the visit occurred at 11:11. I'd actually looked into this before when I had returned home to discover two watches and a kitchen clock all stopped at the exact same time. It was too much of a coincidence to ignore, so I did some research into it. I discovered that eleven is a master number in numerology, signifying intuition, insight, and enlightenment. When paired together with another eleven, it is a clear message from the universe to become conscious and aware. It's also believed to signify the alignment of spiritual awakening, signifying to the person who sees it that they are on the right path and their actions are aligned with their soul's purpose.

It was wonderful to receive all these messages and to know that my husband was still around, walking by our sides even though he wasn't in a physical body. I was totally relaxed about him popping up whenever he could and used to chuckle when the music in my car would randomly change from the ballads I enjoyed to the blaring rock music that Rick always loved. I'd always politely listen to Rick's intervention, smiling all the while, before flicking back to my playlist. I didn't mind a small amount of rock music, but enough is enough.

Rick's regular interventions were more than just a comfort that showed I was not alone and that he was always by my side. They gave me an inner strength too. It was something I was going to need more than ever in the coming weeks because I was about to face learning my biggest lesson yet.

There were signs that the big one had been coming for some time. My automatic writing had been channeling a great deal of very significant messages of late. Some were just a few words long, but they all pointed toward a shift in some way. Words such as "keep moving forward" or "new beginnings" and "go within—it is all within" kept popping up. When I meditated, I saw a range of images of faces and things that I didn't entirely understand, but all seemed to point toward some sort of imminent enlightenment.

I realized I would never get the full answer through channeling. Somehow, I would need to find out for myself what it all meant. I would know when it had happened, though, because once I knew, the universe would give me a sign that I had it right. It's all a game, and when you start to see it as such, the fun begins.

Even though I sensed that whatever was coming was big, I played the game on a lesser scale every day. I would ask my angels for little signs to show that they were listening and put them to the test whenever I could.

"Okay, angels, show me the word *treasure* within the next couple of hours," I said one time. I'd always called Rick *treasure*, so it is not as random as it sounds. Less than one hour later, I was watching a YouTube clip about aliens (Don't ask!) when the word *treasure* came up twice.

"Okay, angels, very good. Let's play a little more," I followed up. "Show me a dragon. In fact, no, let's make it more difficult. Show me a blue dragon!"

Within a couple of hours, someone had posted a picture of a dragon on a Facebook group I was running.

"Well done," I said out loud. "But it wasn't blue." I chuckled.

A few hours later when Jack came home from work, he was very keen to show me a trailer for a new game that was coming out for the PS2. You'll probably have already guessed the main protagonist. Yup: a blue dragon.

I knew that these little games were just diversions, though. My spirit guides had something momentous planned for me. I was certain of that. I just couldn't work out what. The more I thought about it, the more I was guided toward one thought. It had something to do with the latest course I had been compelled to sign up for: hypnotherapy. I'd done dozens of courses over the past eighteen months, many of which I would never have considered if I had not been guided to do so. I trusted my guide's judgement entirely but was a little unsure about this one. Apart from anything else, it was a big commitment: one week every month for four months. I'd paid up in advance for this intensive course and committed myself fully to it, but I did hope it was not a complete waste of time.

When the time came to attend the course, I felt unusually jumpy and nervous. I knew then that whatever it was that had been looming large in my subconscious had to do with what was about to happen.

The drive on the approach to the Ashdown Park Hotel in East Sussex where the course was being held was beautiful. As I looked around in wonder at the pristine grounds, I thought: *Well, at least our trainer has most definitely splashed out on his training venue. That* was a good sign. The secluded, tranquil setting with the beautiful and luxurious hotel in the background was so stunning that it helped calm my nerves. Nothing bad could happen there. Driving to a place like this for one week on and off over the coming months would be a pleasure.

I parked and walked into the hotel where I was directed toward a meeting room. I almost began to lose my nerve again as I wandered down the eerie corridor with its high ceilings and carpeted floor. I felt like I was the only one there. Had I made a huge mistake?

"You lost?" said a man in overalls.

I felt it. In so many ways, other than just being unable to find my classroom. Was this the place where I would finally find myself? Was it here that I would put in place the final piece of the puzzle on a journey that had started a year and a half before?

The man had a kind face and obviously seemed to work there. I explained where I was headed, and he kindly showed me to the classroom that would be my workplace for the following week. I saw immediately that I was the last one there, and a dozen people swiveled around in their chairs to look at me. To my relief, they looked friendly.

"Good morning, everyone," said a man at the front of the room. He was about my age, with boyish good looks. "My name is Andrew Parr. Welcome to your hypnotherapy training course."

I admit it, even then I was still feeling skeptical. I had always thought hypnotherapy was a bit ludicrous. I assumed it was all about setting people up to make fools of themselves in front of others. My attitude wasn't just based on hearsay either.

Years earlier, when we were still living in Doha, the British hypnotist Paul McKenna came out to do a show there as part of his tour. Rick and a few of our friends thought it would be a laugh to go along, and we bought tickets. McKenna started the show with a brief suggestibility hand test. Basically, the audience was shown a way to clasp their hands together, and those unable to unlock their hands were more susceptible. And guess who passed with flying colors? Yup, yours truly. Before I knew it, I was being beckoned up onto the stage, along with a couple of the other members of the audience who were also apparently highly suggestible. With the theater lights glaring away in our eyes, the famous hypnotist set to work. I don't remember much about what he said, but one by one, my fellow suggestables were set off in crazy directions. The guy standing next to me was told he had a one-million-pound lottery ticket in his possession, which he seemed to truly believe. Yet, every time he looked back at the ticket he pulled out of his pocket, it turned out to be a ten-pound prize. The look of disappointment on his face was priceless. Yet, the funniest thing about it was that he kept pulling his ticket out of his pocket over and over again. Each time, his look of elation quickly turned to one of abject despair. I couldn't help laughing, although I knew I was about to do something just as, if not more, daft.

Sure enough, when I caught up with Rick and the others during intermission, I had become a rabid teetotaler. I was absolutely infuriated that anyone could even imagine pouring poisonous alcohol down their throats. It utterly disgusted me.

"Hey, are you okay?" my friend Hazel said when she found me wandering around the bar, lecturing the theatergoers about the evils of drink. "Do you remember what happened back there?" Then, with a huge smile on her face, she added: "I'm going to the bar. Would you like a vodka and orange?"

It was the same drink we'd enjoyed on our arrival at the theater not an hour or so earlier.

"No way!" I practically shrieked, looking horrified. "I will drink orange juice, and so should you."

After that, I continued patrolling the bar, telling anyone who would listen that they must throw their drinks away immediately or face the direst consequences to their health. People laughed in my face as I began to list the various ailments caused by alcohol, counting them off on my fingers: liver disease, obesity, depression … I couldn't believe it as they sipped their drinks nonchalantly as I lectured them. What was wrong with them?

Impatient at their lack of action, I decided to take matters into my own hands and stormed up to the bar.

"I need to speak to the manager," I told the somewhat alarmed bartender. "Right now. This bar needs to be closed immediately. It is a matter of public health."

I vaguely remember another of my stage mates yelling in the background something to do with buckling our seat belts because we were all about to land, but it was all a bit of a fog after that.

Everyone had a good laugh when I was brought back from my trance, and I did find it quite funny too. Nevertheless, I wondered why anyone would want to learn how to hypnotize people. It just seemed a bit cruel laughing at another's expense. Of course, I should also add that you are fully in control when under hypnosis and don't have to take on the therapist's suggestions if you don't want to.

I thought about this experience when I was guided to sign up for the month long course. However, I was so committed to following my guidance that I didn't let it put me off. I didn't even do any real research on the course modules. My faith was so strong I just ran with it.

It didn't take me long to realize what I was doing now had nothing to do with the outlandish, crowd-pleasing, high jinks of stage hypnotists. While both are based on hypnosis, or inducing a passive state of mind for better communication between the conscious and subconscious mind, hypnotherapy takes it onto the next stage. It uses hypnosis as a psychological healing process.

"I think I'm in the wrong class. I didn't realize we were learning psychology!" I joked with Andrew a few days into the course.

I was surprised, not to say relieved, that I wouldn't be reliving my somewhat aggressive period of abstinence or any other foolish behavior. Instead, I was learning how hypnotherapy techniques can really help people make positive changes within themselves. The idea behind it is to reprogram damaging patterns of behavior within the mind. I was fascinated that it was possible to overcome irrational fears, negative thoughts, phobias, and suppressed emotions in this way.

As children, we absorb so much from our parents, family members, friends, and teachers. Some of it good, and some of it bad. These experiences are all subconsciously locked into our brains and are then carried into adulthood. The bad stuff—our deep-seated, inner-child wounds—reemerges in adulthood, manifesting itself in a host of ways, from low self-esteem to eating disorders to intimacy problems to identity problems, to name but a few.

Each day, as the course developed and I learned more, it all made so much sense. So much of what was being said resonated with my own experiences and the experiences I knew about in my friends and family. I was so excited that if I gained a better understanding of hypnotherapy, it may turn out to be a new way of helping people.

Interestingly, I didn't for one moment look upon it as a possible way to help myself. I thought I had done little else but bare my soul for the past eighteen months. I really didn't think there was anything else to come out, and I had healed as much as there was to heal.

I was, of course, wrong.

We were just finishing up a practical exercise, and I was feeling a little cross with myself because I felt I could have done it better. I had gotten into the habit after each session of going through other questions that perhaps could have been asked to take the client to a deeper level of hypnosis in the hope that I could delve into the subconscious and rake through all the stuff that needed to be released. It was annoying that I hadn't done this at all on this occasion, particularly because I'd known what to do, but it just hadn't come out right.

"How did it go?" Andrew asked cheerily.

He was making his usual rounds of the various groups to chat one-to-one about any issues we were having.

Another student and I were seated outside in the garden. It was a beautiful day, so we'd decided to go outside while we tried to see what my blocks were.

"Not brilliant," I said with a resigned shrug. "I'm getting a bit frustrated that whenever I think about standing up to speak to people publicly, to stand on a stage, or even to talk to a tiny group, I freeze. I know what I want to talk about and it's coming from my heart, so there shouldn't be a block, but there is."

Andrew was listening intently and then stood in silence looking at me.

"Why do you think there is a block?" he asked after a thoughtful pause.

"I don't know," I said. And I really didn't. "I can't think why. There shouldn't be any reason. I'm a confident person, so why can't I do it?"

Andrew didn't say anything straight away. He looked like he was weighing up what to say next, so I jumped in and filled the silence.

"I'm really not bothered by others judging me," I said rapidly. "I don't give a toss if people like me or even care that much about their opinions."

He returned a distinctive I'm-not-sure-about-that look at my confession. By now, I was feeling a little self-conscious, despite my bluster.

"Okay, if you could think what the reason was, what would it be?" Andrew asked.

"I don't know. Maybe because I don't think I am wor—" I stopped abruptly.

"Yes, say what you were about to say," Andrew jumped in.

"No, I'm not saying it because that's not how I feel," I replied. My head was spinning a little now.

He was staring at me hard. "Say what you need to say."

"Okay, I don't feel like I am worthy," I said quietly, my head bowed.

"There you go," he replied. "You can stop lying to yourself now."

I didn't say anything for a few moments. I felt a little shocked as I stood there contemplating what had just surfaced. I had just admitted that I didn't feel worthy of being on a stage. Once I said it, I knew it was true. It had always been true. Who would want to listen to what I had to say? Who was I to think that was where I belonged?

Before I could stop myself, I burst into tears—not the sort of light tears that trickle down your cheeks either. There were torrents of them accompanied by deep, rasping sobs.

"It's okay. Just allow it to come," he said

"I'm really sorry," I gulped between sobs. I was surprised by my outburst. "I need to go for a walk."

I wandered off, down the grass banks and into the glaring sunshine. *What had just happened?* I wiped my tears on my sleeve and walked determinedly toward the pond in the center of the grounds. I had to compose myself. I sensed there was more and wasn't sure I was ready for it. But, whether or not I wanted it, it was happening. I needed to try and rationalize it all before I went back into the room.

It took me a little while to sort myself out, but somehow, I managed it. I headed back to the main hotel building and stopped at one of the plush bathrooms to wash my face. Peering at myself in one of the brightly lit mirrors, I saw that I did look a bit of a state.

"Come on, get a grip," I chided myself.

No one said anything as I got back into the classroom, which was a bit of a relief. Everyone just gave me reassuring smiles and nods as I settled back into the chair. I hadn't been the only one to release such emotions. It seemed we were all taking it in turns throughout that week. Even so, I did feel a little embarrassed, and as I sat down, I realized I may have come back in too quickly. I felt like I was in shock. My head was spinning with questions. I just couldn't comprehend that all of this had been tucked down, deep in my subconscious, yet was regularly popping out to dent my confidence just when I needed it most. I had never been aware of it at all, only the *results* of it being there.

"I'm really sorry, Andrew, but I think I need to go home," I said. "I don't know ..." My voice trailed off. I really didn't know. Anything.

Andrew nodded. "'I completely understand. Of course you can go. But I want you to continue to deal with what is going on."

I nodded, although I had no idea what dealing with it really meant. Where would I even start?

"You have many more tears that need to come out," Andrew said, as though he had just read my thoughts.

"Cry," he added. "Let it out."

And that is exactly what I did. Nonstop. For the next two days.

It was a terrible, terrible couple of days. I felt more vulnerable and out of control that at any time in my adult life. I knew immediately where this had all come from too. My parents had divorced when I was nine, and it wasn't easy for any of us—my siblings or my parents. I know my mother and father did the best they could to protect us at the time, but they never really had control of the situation. My nine-year-old self had had to do what it could to protect itself and survive even though at the time I would have had no idea why I had to do this or the deep insecurities it was creating within me.

I needed to let go of this. I did as Andrew said and cried. It felt like I was literally washing away the bad feelings that had laid inside me for so many years. When I finally stopped crying and knew for sure that it had gone, it was an amazing release to be free of it all at last.

It's odd. I had never been one for crying in the past. I used to see it as a sign of weakness. This has now changed. After my awakening, pretty much anything can move me to tears—gratitude; beautiful, angelic, unconditional love; a soppy movie; anything. And I don't mind at all. I am happy to feel and understand the depth of my emotions.

Naturally, when I returned to the hypnotherapy course and explained what had happened to everyone, the tears started again. I must have looked faintly ridiculous, smiling and crying all at the same time, while also expressing profound gratitude to Andrew for helping me release my inner-child baggage.

"You are a beautiful soul," I gulped. "With such a caring nature. You always just listen, which is a skill so few people have, and you never judge. You have helped me so much, and for that, I will be eternally grateful."

My guides had most definitely been on a mission to take me back to my authentic self, releasing me of the worldly baggage most people live with today, and Andrew had been the perfect conduit to achieve this. It was the culmination of an eighteen-month journey, step-by-step, ridding me of emotions that did me no good or held me back. If I had done the course at the beginning of the journey, I have no doubt that the outcome would have been very different. I was not ready then. I was now and had so much gratitude for where this awakening had taken me. This was not just for me either. I would now be able to help so many more people in months and years to come.

As I left the Ashdown Park Hotel for the final time, the four-week course sadly over, I realized I felt completely free inside. It was an incredibly uplifting and hugely spiritual feeling. My spiritual journey was not over. It would never be over. But my soul had found its place in the world, and for the first time in a long while, I felt completely content.

Saoirse Brown

Chapter 12

▬ ▬ ▬ ▬ ▬ ▬ ▬ ▬ ▬ ▬ ▬ ▬ ▬ ▬

MINDFULNESS

For a while I was happy just being. I had found out so much about myself that I needed time to let it settle. I took some weeks out to reconnect with friends and catch up on what had been happening in the months when I had been running from one course to the next.

Spiritualism was never far away, though. And I always enjoyed the meetings I had with like-minded friends when I could discuss where we were spiritually and share experiences. Many books would be suggested for me to read, but I already knew what was in some of them as I'd had the same experiences, so I didn't feel it necessary to buy them.

People would ask, "How do you know that if you haven't read the book?"

"I know what I know," I would say with a smile.

Christmas was fast approaching, and I decided it would be a repeat of last year. My family would be invited, as would my lovely Age Concern lady Hazel. As for New Year's, I would stay home once again, having a quiet evening in after an early dinner with the Ellie and Jack.

Instinctively, I knew New Year's was the time to reflect and work out: What next? I had learned so much, and it was time to pass on the gifts I had received and help others in the best way I could.

When the time came, I discovered very little reflection was required after all. As usual, I was guided to the answer. I'd had it in my mind to become a mindfulness coach. Mindfulness was one of the many courses I had taken on my voyage of discovery. Yet, as I weighed it up, I wondered how I could ignore what I had learned about spiritualism. Surely, this should be a big part of what I did as I went forward.

I ran through the counterarguments in my head. Many people are skeptical about spiritualism. Somehow, they find it much easier to accept mindfulness as a way to correct any imbalance in their lives. Yet, as I knew only too well, if you embrace spiritualism, it opens up a wealth of possibilities. One's personal well-being can be transformed.

In the end, it was a no-brainer: do both. I couldn't do one without the other, so why tie myself in knots trying to separate them? Fear of being judged was something I had discounted months ago.

I launched my online spiritual group alongside my mindfulness coaching business. By intertwining the two, I knew I would be able to help others learn to live a meaningful life full of love, peace, and happiness. My message was simple: It is too easy to rush through life without stopping to notice what is going on around us. We live in a world where we are always focusing on the past or the future, never in the now. That had to change.

Better to live a short life doing what you enjoy than spend lots of years living doing what you don't enjoy!

One of my first clients was a perfect example of this. I had started our session with a nice mindfulness exercise focusing on negativity or positivity. Handing her a pen and paper, I asked her to write down exactly what had happened that morning before she'd come to see me.

"Start from when you woke up and go on to what you did as you began to go about your day," I said.

I gave her two minutes to complete the exercise and watched as she scribbled down a list. When she'd finished, she handed me the list, and I saw a neat column of seven items. I read it aloud.

1) Woke up to the alarm, for which I use my mobile.
2) Go downstairs, make a coffee.
3) Read the paper.
4) Tidy the kitchen, empty bins, etc.
5) Walk the dog.
6) Take a shower.
7) Drive to work.

Interesting.

I handed the paper back to my client.

"Can I ask you to tell me which of the activities you find nourishing and which you find depleting?"

She glanced at the list.

"Well, the alarm is depleting for sure," she said. "Since I use my mobile, I always flick straight over to my emails, and there are usually one or two there from work, which really annoys me."

"And that gets everything off to a bad start?" I interrupted. "Maybe it is better to use a regular alarm clock and leave the work emails until you get to the office?"

She nodded and glanced back at her list.

"I always find reading the newspapers negative and depressing," she said with a what-can-you-do shrug.

"But do you have to read the newspapers?" I pressed.

She shook her head. "No, not really. It's a habit more than anything else—something I have always done."

Back to the list.

"Ah, yes. Tidying the kitchen and emptying the bin is definitely not my favorite activity," she laughed. "Depleting. Definitely."

"Well, obviously that is something that needs to be done," I said, thinking of my own cleaning obsession, which I had never completely shaken, despite my spirit guide's intervention. "But maybe you could try and think about it differently."

"'What do you mean?'"

"If you don't empty the bins, your kitchen will end up smelling. So, instead of seeing this chore as a negative one, why not try and view it positively. By emptying the bin, you are keeping your house smelling nice."

"I suppose so," she replied.

She sounded unsure, but I could see she was thinking about it seriously. That small change in how she viewed the event would make a world of difference once she tried it.

"And the drive to work: nightmare," my client concluded, putting the list down beside her. "There is too much traffic on the road, and it is too stressful."

"Okay, I understand that, and there is not much you can do about the cars on the road," I said. "But how about leaving fifteen minutes earlier, so you are not always trying to beat the clock? Or, maybe try a more scenic route? You could do that if you gave yourself time."

As she listened, I could see that I had made a breakthrough. She immediately looked, well, lighter of being.

"There is always a positive to a negative," I said, pushing the point home. "We just need to find it."

It's true too. There is so much of what we do throughout the day that doesn't bring us happiness and can be changed, usually without too much effort.

One of the most important changes we can all make is to stop focusing on the future and waiting for things to happen. It is a mindless distraction and stops you from enjoying the here and now. We're all guilty of it: always looking forward to the weekend when you think you'll be able to finally relax. Why not find some time for yourself right now? Today? Or, why are you putting off booking a much-needed break until your bonus is announced (when it might not happen at all)? Find another way to make that booking. Or, what is the point of waiting until you are forty/fifty/sixty (delete as appropriate) before you start that book you've always said you are going to write? Start today. Right now. Type one word and then the next, and it will soon add up to a page, then a chapter, and then a full book.

If you are constantly thinking about tomorrow, before you know it, you will have wished your life away and never really lived a life at all. Too many people forget to enjoy the life they have as it unfolds right in front of them. When you live a life like this, you are literally telling the universe that you are not ready to live a fulfilled life, so that is exactly what you finish up with: an unfulfilled life. This kind of thinking is just a habit—one that needs to be broken. Stop waiting for life to begin and recognize that it is already well on the way. Enjoy it!

An important part of this process is to reconnect our bodies with the sensations we experience. This means waking up to the feelings, thoughts, sights, sounds, smells, and tastes of the present moment. We're too ready to live in our heads, having our thoughts drive our emotions and behaviors. With a little bit of work and commitment, we can gradually train ourselves to notice when our thoughts are taking over.

Most of us have issues that we find hard to let go of, and mindfulness can help us deal with them more productively. When you can stand back and observe how you think and feel about situations in your life, it can become easier, and you will begin to see where your thoughts hold you back. It is all about allowing your thoughts and feelings to come and go freely. Observe them without trying to stop them and without making an attachment to them. It also involves acceptance of how we are feeling without judgment. The only way to do this is to train your mind, gradually reducing any negative or unwanted anxieties and worries and replacing them with a positive, peaceful place. This can be achieved through meditation but also by taking time throughout the day to observe what is happening with your thought process and how you deal with certain situations and people.

Your mind is your instrument. Learn to be its master and not its slave.

Throughout my journey over the past couple of years, I have learned to remove myself from my script and observe my life as though I am watching myself in a movie. It's very simple technique to do, and it really helps. If you think of your life in this way, it is then possible to direct the movie and make the decisions you need to make the movie, one you want to star in. *You* put *you* where *you* want to be. You are in charge of your own life, you have choices, and you can make anything happen. It's all about manifesting your desires.

I always tell people to have a look at others who surround them and to ask: Are they positive people? Then ask yourself: Are you happy living where you are living? Are you happy in your job? Are you happy in your relationship? Look and see what you would like to change. Is there somebody in your life you have conflict with? Why do you think that is, without attaching the blame to someone else? Be honest with yourself.

Another important question to ask yourself is what do you see in others that seems to trigger something in you? We all mirror one another, and this is where lessons can be learned very quickly. You cannot love or hate something about another person unless it reflects to you something you love or hate about yourself. This is something I learned through my interaction with Simon. Once you recognize how you reflect what you see in others, it makes everything a lot easier to understand and deal with. We are all enrolled in a full-time, informal school called life. People are in your life for a reason—for you to learn lessons—and these lessons will be repeated until you have graduated and moved on to another.

While all this is going on, give yourself time to be kind to yourself. Self-love and compassion is crucial. We need to give ourselves the same kindness and care that we would give to a good friend in need. For example, if someone you care for tells you that she is upset because she has put on weight, you would respond in a kind, caring, supportive manner. You need to be able to give yourself the same treatment. Instead of beating yourself up over those few extra pounds with brutal self-criticism, acknowledge that it is okay, just like you would to a friend. It is all too easy to mentally punish ourselves when it really isn't necessary. Get to know yourself without being judgmental and fully accept yourself as you are. Remind yourself that you are valuable, deserve happiness, are worthy, and are already perfect. When you begin to love yourself unconditionally, that love and compassion just naturally oozes out to others.

A more spiritual approach to life complements the mindfulness perfectly. Before my spiritual awakening, I never stopped. I was awake at five o'clock in the morning to go out and walk the dog, and my house would be spotlessly cleaned by eight. After that, I would shower and get ready to go wherever I needed to be during the day. I never allowed myself to just sit and be. In fact, I very rarely sat down at all.

My guides and angels have shown me that in order to live a more relaxed, peaceful life, I need to slow down and give myself the time to sit in silence, whether that is through meditation, yoga, or just a quiet walk to bask in nature. In moments of quiet like this, a lot of answers come. It gives you the time to tune in to yourself, dig deep, and know what you truly want out of life. It opens you up to an understanding of what your soul's destiny is and also what your purpose is all about. The answers to life's questions lie inside you. All you need to do is listen, and this will only come in moments of silence.

If your mind is peaceful, you will be happy and free from worries, regardless of external conditions. If your mind is not peaceful, you will find it very difficult to be happy, regardless of what you have externally. Wealth or material items will not fill this void.

I have, on many occasions, been told not to chase money. Of course, that is easy to say but not all that easy to abide by because it is nice to have something in the bank. However, I have found that if you relax and don't chase it, money will come to you, one way or another. I was shown this through my experiences of day trading, which were a classic example of this. If I sit and anxiously watch the markets going up and down, I lose more often than not. The days I put a trade on and then get busy with other things and forget all about it, I usually make money. Strange but true.

I've seen it elsewhere in my life too. I'd advertised a computer chair on eBay. It used to be in Rick's room, but after a quick freshen up of the décor there, I decided I would like a smaller chair. It was up for sale for quite some time, but despite my constantly checking, no one made a bid. I ended up putting it into the garage and forgetting about it. Then, out of nowhere, I received an email asking me if it was still for sale. The inquirer asked if, instead of paying the forty pounds that it was advertised for, would I accept thirty pounds? I replied with a: "Yes, when can you collect?" The buyer's response was "Tomorrow and I will give you thirty-five pounds." He was offering me more money, even though I had already accepted his first offer.

Put what you would like out to the universe, and it comes back to you in this way. I did the same with my gym membership when it was up for renewal and they emailed to say as much. I had an internal debate because it was an expensive gym and I hadn't been as much as I would have liked. So, I put it out there. I told the universe that I would rejoin if they gave me one month free. Within a couple of hours, someone called me from the gym to say if I rejoined they would give me one month free. It is absolutely crazy what you can manifest.

In every area, whether it is money, relationships, or day-to-day drudgery that drives you mad, the more relaxed you are and happy to just let things happen, the easier life becomes.

I've used many of the spiritual and mindfulness techniques that I speak of in the writing of this very book. When I first began to think about it, I was guided to make a vision board, outlining my ambition to pass on what I had learned via the printed word. I confess, I had never really rated the idea of vision boards before, thinking them to be somewhat wishful and most likely filled with out-of-reach ideas. Nevertheless, I made one. I couldn't believe that almost immediately things began to be crossed off. As the weeks went by, I secured an agreement with Balboa Press to publish my book. I was blown away. They were on my vision board, and all it took was one phone call. The only downside was that the cost to publish it was going to be over my budget, but I knew it was something I had to do.

"Don't worry about money. You are being guided. Go with it," I said to myself.

I made the payment, knowing that things would work out for me financially. I knew because the universe had said so. The next day my accountant phoned me to say there was extra money in the kitty and asked if I would like it transferred to my bank. The amount covered the publishing costs, with an extra twelve hundred pounds left over. The universe was really looking out for me.

I had been advised by an editor friend to read more memoirs before I started writing my own book. He said this would give me an idea of the different writing styles I might use and may stir up some inspiration within me too. Within a couple of days of hearing that, three people came to me with memoirs clasped in their hands, asking if I would like to read them. A few years ago, I might have found this very bizarre, but I now accept that the universe is here to help me move forward and support me by sending people in my path.

This communication is open to every one of us if we just take the time to listen. As I've been constantly reminded throughout this journey: two ears, one mouth.

I am hoping that by writing this book I will help people who are going through grief. I want them to know that there is a light at the end of the tunnel. If my words give comfort to those who have lost loved ones and help them to know that, although our dearest leave us at a physical level, their spirits stay with us and .

watch over us, then I will have achieved what I set out to do. Through a mindful approach to living, we can bring about peace and happiness within ourselves. All we need to do is to become conscious of our thoughts, and we will start to eliminate all worries and anxieties we live with.

Afterword

■ ■ ■ ■ ■ ■ ■ ■ ■ ■ ■ ■ ■

WHERE AM I NOW?

May 30, 2018. Two years to the day of my amazing husband making his transition.

Without a doubt, I have learned more in the past two years than I have learned during my entire lifetime put together. It has been a very painful journey but also wonderful at the same time. I now know that life truly is about finding yourself, and during this process, I have done just that. I no longer need anything external to bring about my happiness. I am free from that. I have all of what I need within.

Life is all about love. A connection to all that is a oneness with God, Holy Spirit, source, divine energy, the universe, whatever you are comfortable calling it. I will never truly be able to put into words my connection with angels. All I can say is that they are around, letting me know that they are there. A gentle rubbing on the top of my head lets me know their presence. Their love so unconditional it is overwhelming.

My husband has never left me, just his physical body. I have been guided, carried, and cradled throughout this process. Rick continues to walk alongside me, making sure I get where I need to be. I have been shown the tools to help others achieve the same. Friends and

155

family have questioned the money I have spent on courses, more out of concern about me wasting money due to grief, although I know their worries are well-meaning and are fueled by love and concern for me. But, knowing what I know now, I would have spent ten times that amount to have this feeling. The power I have is within me, knowing that I am part of God, the universe, source and that nothing is ever out of my reach is indescribable. We all have this power within us.

If I was asked to try and describe my life since my husband's passing, I would say it was as though I have been handed a giant gift. It is almost like I am playing pass the parcel all by myself. I am repeatedly being handed this gift to continue opening, and each time I do, such wonder falls out of each box. I am in awe of what the universe provides, if only you allow it. We fight so hard against life, when in reality there really is nothing to do but just allow life to flow through us.

Although I am truly blessed to be able to receive these messages, I am not unique. We all have the ability to do so, but the awareness of it, or desire to acknowledge it, is cruelly knocked out of us at a young age. For reasons I can't fathom, we are conditioned to live a certain way and conform to what society believes to be acceptable.

Deceased loved ones are always trying to communicate with us. But more often than not, we dismiss anything out of the ordinary as mere a coincidence. Perhaps there is a belief that any connection to our spirit guides simply couldn't be that easy. But it is. Once you begin to follow those small bread crumbs that are scattered for you and open your mind and heart to what is being shown to you, you will begin to understand that those you believe you have lost are still there for you, loving and guiding you along. Even if you are still a little cynical, ask yourself, what have you got to lose by playing along with them?

It may help to cast your mind back to the time when you were a child—the time when your imagination was truly free and you lapped up stories about worlds you had never seen and didn't truly

Saoirse Brown

understand. When you closed your eyes, you'd be able to whisk yourself off anywhere in the universe and beyond. Start living through children's eyes again. Believe that magical things do happen, and then watch them unfold. Pull down the barriers that adults like to erect around anything that isn't instantly explainable and open yourself up to childlike wonder. You'd be amazed at what you will see when you truly open your eyes.

Since my childhood, I have always dreamt of seeing spirits and being able to pass on messages to grieving relatives and friends. I know it was a gift I always had, and it was Rick's passing that awoke it within me and allowed me to see it properly. I also realize that my initial awakening, where I could only see energy, was actually just the beginning. Now that I am completely open to everything I see, my experiences have become so much more intense and I understand so much more.

Just a few days before Rick's birthday, I was sitting in his room. I still call it that, even today and even though it has been decorated in a different way to accommodate my office furniture and therapy couch. Sonia had come to visit, and we were sitting and talking to each other when strange things started to occur. We both had goose bumps up and down our bodies at exactly the same time. Instinctively, I swung my head around to look over at the door, and there, leaning against the door frame, was my beautiful husband. He was wearing his normal attire, golf T-shirt and jeans, and just watching us with a smile on his face. I can barely describe the feeling of love and happiness that surged through my whole body at that moment.

On the anniversary of Rick's passing a few weeks later, I began the morning by walking over to the large picture I have of him in my bedroom. I wished him a happy birthday. For me, it's his birthday; there is no death. And I kissed the picture. I still talk to him on a daily basis and ask questions. The answers always come, one way or another. He decided that, for this particular day, he would like to give me another gift. I have stopped saying that there is no need to give me anything and his presence is enough. Although, if I am honest, I do rather like them.

I headed out to beautiful Headley in Surrey, I walked my gorgeous dog Maisy on the Natural Trust Land there most days. When I pulled up my car, it was deathly quiet, which was hardly surprising because it was only six o'clock in the morning, and nobody was around. I let Maisy out of the car, and as usual, I was in a relaxed state, enjoying the sensation of just being at one with nature and tuning into the joyous sounds of the birds that were heralding the new day with a magnificent chorus. Suddenly, a sound alerted me to the fact that I wasn't alone. I swung around sharply to sense a large black Labrador running toward me, his tongue lolling out of his mouth, panting.

Oh, there is someone else here after all, I thought to myself.

I glanced back at Maisy who was standing just twelve feet away, stock still and staring. My body was covered in goose bumps as I looked down at the magnificent Labrador, that was now sitting at my feet, looking at me with love and acceptance. I started to cry. I knew that, physically, there was no dog there, but the spirit of this beautiful dog was such a powerful presence.

"You enjoying your walk?" I said quietly.

The dog continued to pant as I wondered how often he used to come to Headley with his owner. How many times had he enjoyed the walk that Maisy and I loved so much?

"Would you like to walk with us?"

The acknowledgement was enough. The dog turned and ran off.

"Thank you," I murmured to his retreating form.

What a wonderful gift. Thank you, Rick.

Although I know for sure that Rick will continue to guide me as long as he thinks I still need him, in recent weeks he has begun to tell me to move on. Not to forget him. I would never do that. But to live my life and to fulfill my purpose without constantly looking back. As always, Rick showed me this in the gentlest, yet most elegant way.

For all the years of our marriage, I didn't wear my wedding ring very often. I would only really put it on for special occasions or if we went out for dinner. Rick wasn't much into rings either. In fact, he had lost his wedding ring about a year after we were married. I did try to get him to let me replace it, but as he wasn't much of a ring person, he wasn't having any of it. I used to tease him and say he sold it so that he didn't have to wear one.

I didn't have an engagement ring until a few years ago because we'd got married in such a hurry. Rick had often asked me if I wanted one, and I had always replied that I'd rather wait until I found the perfect one, which I was certain I would know once I saw it. Somehow, it took twenty years for that moment. I already had the carat weight I would like in my mind, which was 1.56 and that it would be a round solitaire diamond. I had no idea where that notion had come from—well, at least not at the time. Then, not long before we had returned to England, we had decided to visit a new shopping mall in Dubai and chanced upon a Tiffany store. We stopped to look inside the upmarket jeweler, and there, right in front of us, was a 1.56-carat diamond ring in the exact same shape I had longed for. Rick asked if I would like it.

"It's too expensive," I exclaimed.

"You have waited a long time for an engagement ring. I want to buy it for you," he answered.

We went back and forth for a while, with me refusing and Rick insisting. In the end, he went ahead and bought it anyway.

After Rick passed away, I started wearing an eternity ring on my wedding finger. I wore it whenever I went out. Partly, it was as an accessory, but mostly it was because I didn't want men presuming I was single.

Then the ring disappeared. Completely. It was so odd. I have only ever lost one piece of jewelry before this, and that was when I was eighteen. My dad had bought me a mixed gold bracelet for my birthday, and it vanished somehow. These days, though, I never lost anything. I am supremely tidy and organized and know where everything is in my home—everything. It was just so odd. I knew exactly when I had worn it before, so where had it gone? For whatever reason, I knew Rick had taken it. It was his signal that he wanted me to move on.

He must have sensed I was unsure. It seemed such a big step. Perhaps I was misinterpreting it? So, he sent me another sign that this was his wish.

I was guided to watch a movie. This has happened quite a few times, and I never research what these movies are about. I just know that they need to be watched, and they always give me answers or lessons. There was always a benefit.

To this day, I am blown away with synchronicities shown by this movie. I had to keep rewinding it to check I wasn't imagining it. The plot was about a woman whose husband had recently died. He was in the process of building a time machine and was brutally murdered for sharing too much information about his invention. The husband managed to communicate with his wife via her dreams, showing her how to use the time machine to go back and see what happened to him. Somehow, she manages to do this and is able to witness everything for herself. She travels back and forth as the plot develops, yet on one journey, her wedding ring disappears. He was telling her to move on.

The ring story was not the only coincidence with the film. The other ironic thing about this movie was that the dead husband had told his wife to remove her watch and never to wear it again. There have been a couple of occasions, when channeling, that I have been told that it isn't necessary to wear a watch because time doesn't exist. I removed it after a few times of hearing this, although I should add that I rather missed wearing it because I quite liked the design and it is a nice accessory. I decided to start wearing it again, but that said, I never look at the time on it. I also don't adjust the time on my watch or the clocks around the house when the clocks go forward for the spring or back in winter. My friends all laugh about it, but that's just the way I am.

SAOIRSE BROWN

With the movie, Rick proved yet again that nothing is a coincidence. Everything from the people you meet to the things you read to the movies you watch to the words that people say—all of it is there to connect you to something else. My advice to everyone is to observe and learn. All the time.

I have taken my husband's advice and decided it is time. As part of making a new start, I have been guided to put our house on the market. Once it is sold, Ellie, Maisy, and I will find a new home. My gorgeous son, Jack, won't be coming with us. He was ready for a change too. Jack is about to move into a flat with Freya, and they will be starting a new chapter in their lives.

Where will we be going? I have no idea! I will leave it up to the universe to find that place for us. I know that what I have been given the past couple of years has been beyond my wildest dreams, but I also know that there are even better things to come. I know too that when the time is right, my ring will return.

My life is unfolding as I have manifested it to. All the desires that I have posted on my vision board are being crossed off on a monthly basis. The main purpose for my life now centers around volunteering. I decided not long after Rick passed away that I would like to offer my guest bedroom for anyone who was visiting the Royal Marsden for treatment or a family member. An illness such as cancer and the treatment required is terrible enough to have to deal with, without the financial burden of taking time off work and paying for hotel accommodation. My business card sits there at the hospital for such a case. Anyone who requires this help will be shown it by the universe. The people who need you will always find you.

My other big desire, which I recently began, is to help with hospice patients in the community. If I can add a little sunshine into the remaining days of these patients, then it makes it all worth my while. My other volunteer work will continue as usual.

As for the rest, well, again I have no idea. I no longer ask why, when, or how. Things are just as they are meant to be. I don't need all the answers. I allow things to fall into place and just be. It's the easiest way I have ever lived. I have love, peace, and happiness and need nothing external to that. Whatever comes my way will be perfect, just as it should be, for whatever reason.

Along this journey I have met some beautiful souls—some who have just come in for a short period of time, helped me with one thing or another, and then left, and others who have played a longer-term role. Everyone has been equally important, and I am eternally grateful to each and every one. It is all about lessons and tests, and the sooner you are able to accept and see how this all works, the easier life becomes.

I look forward to continuing on, opening this large gift I have been given, and sharing it with others.

Bibliography

Redfield, James. *The Celestine Prophecy* (London, Bantam, 1994).

Renard, Gary R. *The Disappearance of the Universe: Straight Talk about Illusions, Past Lives, Religion, Sex, Politics and the Miracles of Forgiveness* (Carlsbad, CA: Hay House, 2004).

Printed in the United States
By Bookmasters